HARAB SERAPEL

~ Ravens Of The Burning God ~

By

~ S. Ben Qayin - Edgar Kerval ~

Copyright

Copyright S. Ben Qayin. All rights reserved. No part of this publication may be reproduced, distributed or transmitted in any form or by any means, without the prior written permission of the author, except for brief quotations in critical reviews and other noncommercial use.
First Edition: 2020

Disclaimer

Personal success depends on work ethic, so results will vary. Consider all information adult knowledge and not legal or medical advice. Use this at your own risk. Do not violate local, national, or international laws. If any problems occur, contact a licensed psychologist or doctor immediately. S. Ben Qayin is not responsible for consequences of actions. This book is for readers of age 18 or older.

Credits

Author: *S. Ben Qayin*
Foreword: *Asenath Mason*
Artwork:

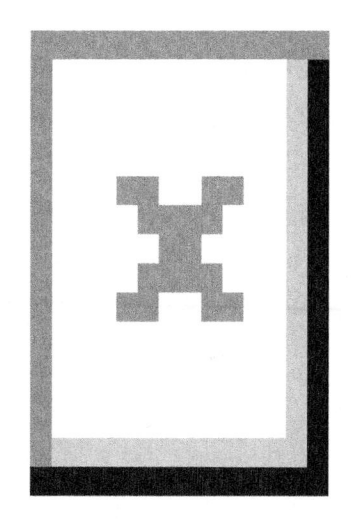

The Raven

*...Dissolution in the claws of time,
sublime chants of dispersion
putrefaction in many masks,
decomposition in many paths
a green emerald torch burning beyond
the whispers of the
realms of death...*

~ Edgar Kerval

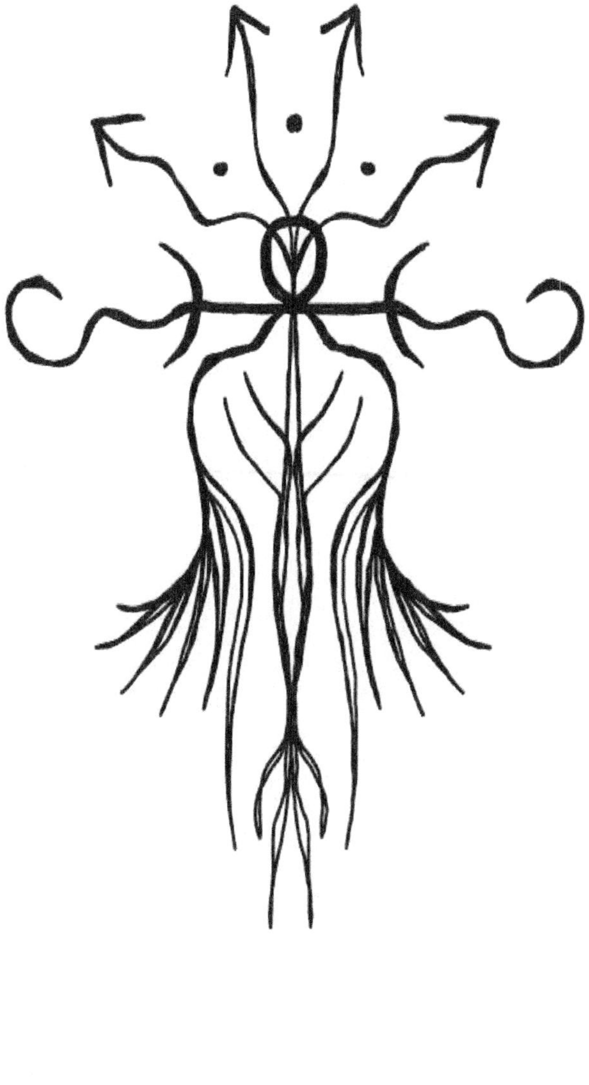

Noah's Raven

"Why should I have returned?
My knowledge would not fit into theirs.
I found untouched the desert of the unknown,
Big enough for my feet. It is my home.
It is always beyond them. The future
Splits the present with the echo of my voice.
Hoarse with fulfillment, I never made
promises." ~ W.S. Merwin

Contents

~ Foreword By Asenath Mason

<u>Written By S. Ben Qayin:</u>

~ Introduction

~ Into the Sitra Ahra

~ Getzphiel; The Burning God

~ The Invocation of Getzphiel

~ The Ravens of Dispersion; Wrath of the Unkindness

~ Rite of The Ravenous Ravens

~ The Ravens of Devouring Death

~ Ba'el-A'arab-Zaraq; King of Hell, Lord of Darkness

~ The Raising of Ba'el-A'arab-Zaraq

~ Halahel; Unholy Darkness with the Eyes of an Angel

~ The Conjuration of Halahel

Written By Edgar Kerval:

~ Through The Claws of Eternity

~ The Rite of the Black Mirror

~ The Negativity of Netzach and Darkside of Venus

~ The fetish Totem of Arab Zaraq (Consecration Rite)

~ The Sanctuary of the Raven's flesh (Invocation)

~ The Obsidian Gate and the Nigredo Phase

~ Theriomorphic shadow of Baa'l I Zaraq

~ Explorations of Tunnels of Niantiel & Kurgasiax

~ Final Word: The Sphere of Uncontrolled Intent

Illustrations

Plate 1-Black Raven by Sean Woodward

Plate 2-Solace of Kurgasiax By Matt Baldwin Ives

Plate 3-Qayin messor coronatus et magnus ben samael by itan Celebrinbor

Plate 4-Ravens by N.N

Plate 5-The Mask of Arab Zaraq By Kaela

Plate 6-The Shadow of Arab Zaraq by Jhonatan Nicosia

Plate 7-Corridors of Niantiel by Matt Baldwin- Ives

Plate 8-Die Zersetzer by Sean Woodward

Plate 9-Harab Serapel Collaboration Matt Baldwin- Ives & Giselle Bolotin

Plate 10-Baal by Serpents Soul Art

Plate 11-Baal I Zaraq by Jhonatan Nicosia

Plate 12-Sevenfold by N.N

Plate 13-Master of the Qliphoth by Sean Woodward

Plate 14- Venus Decomposing by Matt Baldwin Ives

Solace Of Kurgasiax

Preface

You are holding in your hands a grimoire dedicated to the gnosis of A'arab Zaraq, or *"Raven of Dispersion"*. Of all the Qliphoth below the Abyss, A'arab Zaraq occupies a special place because it completes the initiatory process of the astral plane, the ordeal that is crucial to the whole spiritual growth according to the map of the Dark Tree. Little is known about this mysterious realm from Qabalistic literature, though. If we refer to older sources we will only find an information that A'arab Zaraq is the dark counterpart of the Sephira Netzach on the Tree of Life and constitutes the opposite or antithesis of its bright equivalent. Netzach is a part of the Pillar of Mercy and translates to "victory" or "eternity." Its virtues are endurance, unselfishness, and perpetuity, its ruling planet is Venus, and its spiritual experience is the Vision of Beauty Triumphant. The title of its dark counterpart is the Ravens of Dispersion or the Ravens of the Burning of God, and its initiatory forces are believed to be demons in the form of hideous ravens issuing from a volcano.

The image of a raven is ambiguous in itself. It is a scavenger often seen on battlefields picking at the remains of corpses of people and animals alike, which is connected with A'arab Zaraq as well, showing that we are dealing here with the battlefield ruled by the fearsome god of war, Baal. The association of the raven with this Qlipha is also derived from story included in the Bible, in which Noah sent a raven from his ark to confirm the receding floodwaters. The bird, however, saw a lot of corpses to feed on and never returned to the ark. Then Noah sent a dove with the same mission, and the dove, a creature representing purity, could not find a resting place among decaying corpses and returned to signal the end of the flood. In the Qabalah, both these birds are connected with the symbolism of Netzach/A'arab Zaraq, the dove on its bright side, the raven representing the deadly forces of death and dispersion.

The raven as a symbol is a mystical bird. In many ancient cultures ravens were harbinger of omens and prophecies, messengers between worlds, especially the world of humans and the realm of spirits. One of the most profound myths of ravens as intermediaries between the worlds is the story of the Norse god Odin, who was always accompanied by two ravens: Hugin who represented the power of thought and active pursuit of knowledge, and Munin, representing the mind and intuition. Odin would send the two ravens out each day to fly above the earth, and when the day ended, they would return to him and tell him all they had seen and learned on their journeys. The same function we find in the Raven of Dispersion - the forces of this Qlipha carry the initiate between the realms: astral and solar, into the heart of the whole tree, acting as mediators and guides into deep mysteries of the Qliphoth. Therefore, the raven's resting place is both A'arab Zaraq and Thagirion, the central Qlipha on the tree. Also, in spite of its black feathers, the raven is traditionally a solar bird, associated with Athena and Apollo, deities of light and the sun, illumination and wisdom. On the other hand, it is also symbolic of the shadow self, and in this case, integration of the conscious and unconscious within the adept, which is initiated on the astral plane and eventually comes to completion in the realm of the Black Sun. Inner secrets are unveiled, darkness is brought to the light of consciousness, and the shadow self is confronted and embraced in the initiatory process of the Qliphoth.

All this and a lot more is offered to us by the Raven of Dispersion. Ruled by Baal, the god of war, Venus Illegitima, the dark lady of passions, and Tubal Cain, the maker of sharp weapons, this realm stands for change and transformation in a violent and dynamic way. It will prompt you to change and movement in your life, rebirth if you find yourself in need of spiritual rejuvenation, or renewal when your life seems stagnant and you cannot move forward. Its forces will lift you up and carry you on the wings of the raven through your personal darkness toward illumination within. This change, however, occurs through facing various battles in your life. Just like Netzach is *"Victory"*, here you have to be victorious as well - in conquering your fear, hesitation, stagnation, and everything that keeps you within your safety zone. Barriers will be dispersed, and you will become equipped with the sharp weapons of Tubal Cain, driven by the raw and passionate energy of Venus, and led by Baal into battle in order to overcome your obstacles and defeat your personal adversaries.

The raven is also a symbolic animal in alchemy, where it represents the first stage of the alchemical process of transmutation. This is the nigredo phase, *"Blackening"*, the stage of decomposition and putrefaction. It is equivalent to the Dark Night of the Soul, where we become exposed to our inner darkness and all that it carries within, when the soul is stripped from all its layers and reconstructed in a new, better form. By exploring the external fire, the inner fire is ignited and the body is reduced to primal matter from which it arose. In spiritual terms, this is the phase in which the initiate reconstructs their personal universe, redefines short and long term goals, and decides what to empower and what to leave behind. The *"Black Crow"* is another name for this process, referring to the symbolism of death and putrefaction. Psychologically, this dark phase is a process of directing ourselves toward self-knowledge. This occurs through the works of the whole astral plane: in the realm of Gamaliel we are guided by our fantasies, in Samael we explore the intellect and its dark side, and in A'arab Zaraq we explore our personal underworld by means of emotions. They can be violent or loving and passionate, originating in the current of Baal and powered up by the sensual energy of Venus. But once we are in the core of our inner darkness, we are able to light the fire within and initiate the next stage of the alchemical process: albedo, *"Whitening"*. We learn how to handle our shadow, instead of letting it control us, which is an essential step in the harsh but fascinating journey through the dark side of the Qabalistic Tree.

This alchemical transmutation through the Raven of Dispersion is also the subject of this grimoire. Written by two experienced authors and magicians, Edgar Kerval and S. Ben Qayin, it provide a unique perspective on the Qlipha and its initiatory mysteries. Through rites of wrath and fury, as well as death and putrefaction, you will be invited to enter your personal underworld and confront the darkness within. By means of invocations, evocations, and workings of the Other Side, you will be lead into the heart of the volcano, from which you will arise on the black wings of shadow to soar through planes and dimensions as the Raven of Dispersion, in ecstatic flight into the Black Sun. By exploring the fierce path of Baal and the sensual current of Venus, you will be shown how to transform your weakness into strength, fear into courage, and darkness into light, understanding and clarity. This is a beautiful grimoire that will take you to the depths of your soul, shake your universe, and let you become the eye of the storm, where you can find illumination and power.

~ Asenath Mason

Qayin Messor Coronatus

Introduction

> *"Out of the ground the Lord God caused to grow every tree that is pleasing to the sight and good for food; the tree of life also in the midst of the garden, and the tree of knowledge, of good and evil."* ~ Genesis 2:9 - 14

The Tree of Death…of Knowledge…Exists within the hidden shadows of Qabalistic reality, in a realm known as the Sitra Ahra…the vast cold region where Light is but a grey band upon the farthest horizons. The Sitra Ahra is the anathema of creation, for it lies concealed *'behind'* and *'below'* its illuminated counterpart, the realm of holiness and purity.

As a coin has two sides, we see a duality here that exists and is represented in the form of Light and Darkness which oppose one another, but nevertheless are eternally bound as one. This is essentially the philosophy of having two opposing energetic intelligences or forces united under one all-encompassing energetic Qabalistic intelligence known only as *'Ayn'*. We find this duality in unity at the core of not only the Judaic teachings, but also within the traditions of Taoism and Zurvanism as well. This theory is artfully mirrored in the Taijitu symbol known more commonly as the Yin and Yang symbol.

This perspective embodies the idea of the personification of the eternal waring forces of Order and Chaos *(Light and Darkness)*. These forces are as a scale that never finds rest, the balance constantly being shifted from one side to the other. These waring forces of Order and Chaos are evenly matched; One force rises up over aeons of time gaining control, only to have the opposing force in turn rise up to push it back down. One force can never completely dominate the other. It is an eternal ebb and flow, so change can never cease in the Consensual Reality Matrix and experience never end. This cycle is eternal. It is as playing chess against yourself, only to stalemate match after match. The forces of Chaos and Order are equal. Though, calm between these two forces can never be known, now that the proverbial boat has begun to rock, they are set into perpetual motion. It is a game of tug of war that can never be won.

These forces of Chaos and Order are generally assigned the description and position of *'Good and Evil'*. However, this description is made from the viewpoint of one of the two perspectives *(Chaos or Order)*, making it a limited concept. When one views the duality that exists as a whole, counteracting each other equally as one working machine/system/program, one can see that neither of these forces are *'good or evil'*.

When one combines warm water with cold water, neither forces are good or evil. A forest fire could be seen as evil, destroying all life. But, it is needed every so often to cleanse the land and provide nutrients and space for new growth to occur. It is an endless cycle of destruction and rebirth. It is continuous change. It is continuous experience. And truly, neither are good nor bad, for darkness cannot exist without light, and light not without darkness.

This duality is reflected in the natures of the Qabalistic Tree of Life and the Tree of Death. Without going into too much detail *(as I assume one has a general understanding of the concept at this point in one's studies)*, the Tree of Life is a Qabalistic representation of *'being'* and *'creation'*, how existence came to be and its general composition. The Tree of Life includes various attributes at progressing stations, and ruling intelligences of these points. These stations are known as Sephiroth. As stated each Sephira has an attribute such as *'Severity, Compassion, Beauty and Kindness'*. Each Sephira bleed into and influence each other in various ways and combinations. The ten Sephiroth, their attributes and ruling angelic spirits are as follows:

~ <u>Kether</u>: *'The Crown'*

<u>Ruling Angelic Intelligence</u>: *Metatron*

~ <u>Chochmah</u>: *'Wisdom'*

<u>Ruling Angelic Intelligence</u>: *Raziel*

~ <u>Binah</u>: *'Understanding'*

<u>Ruling Angelic Intelligence</u>: *Tzaphqiel*

~ <u>Chesed</u>: *'Kindness'*

<u>Ruling Angelic Intelligence</u>: *Tzadqiel*

~ <u>Gevurah</u>: *'Severity'*

<u>Ruling Angelic Intelligence</u>: *Khamael*

~ Tiferet: *'Beauty'*

Ruling Angelic Intelligence: *Raphael*

~ Netzach: *'Victory'*

Ruling Angelic Intelligence: *Haniel*

~ Hod: *'Splendor'*

Ruling Angelic Intelligence: *Michael*

~ Yesod: *'Foundation'*

Ruling Angelic Intelligence: *Gabriel*

~ Malkuth: *'Kingdom'*

Ruling Angelic Intelligence: *Sandalphon*

~ Da'ath: *'Wisdom'*

Ruling Demonic Intelligence: *Choronzon*

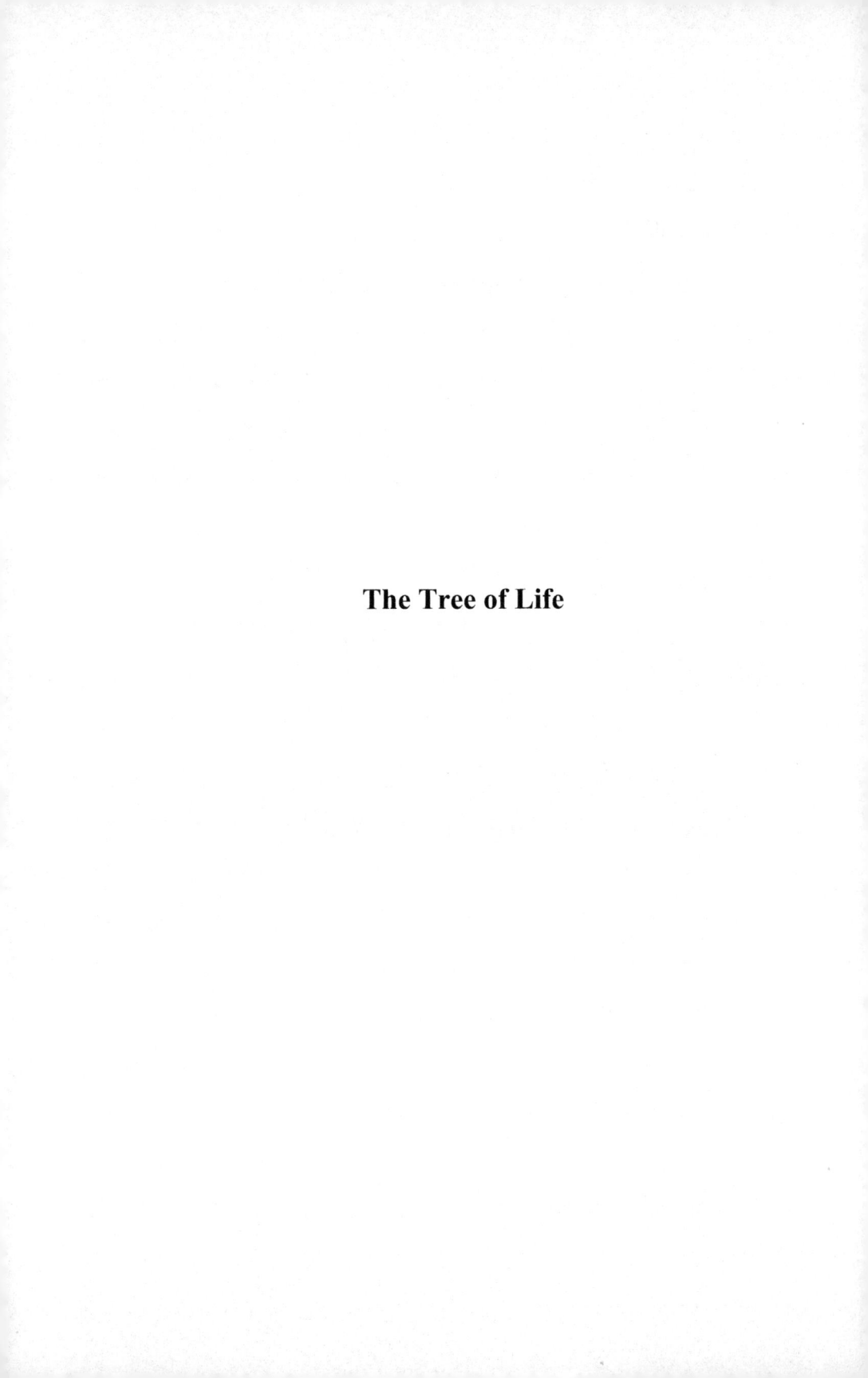

The Tree of Life

KETHER
'The Crown'
Ruling Angelic Intelligence:
Metatron

BINAH
'Understanding'
Ruling Angelic Intelligence:
Tzaphqiel

CHOCHMAH
'Wisdom'
Ruling Angelic Intelligence:
Raziel

DA'ATH
'Wisdom'
Ruling Demonic Intelligence:
Choronzon

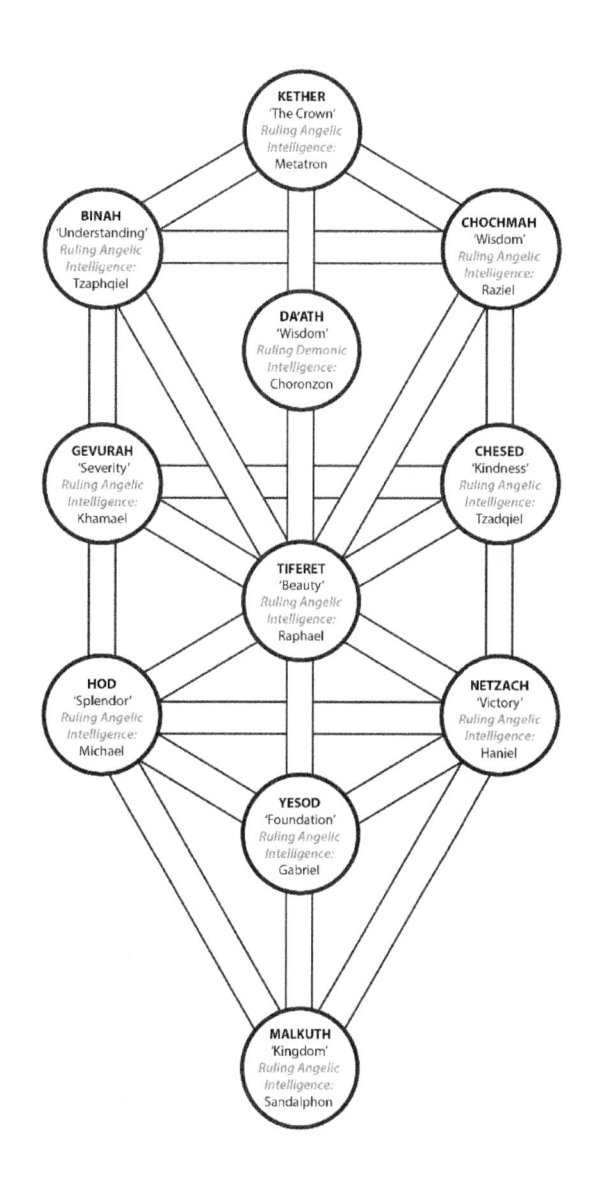

GEVURAH
'Severity'
Ruling Angelic Intelligence:
Khamael

CHESED
'Kindness'
Ruling Angelic Intelligence:
Tzadqiel

TIFERET
'Beauty'
Ruling Angelic Intelligence:
Raphael

HOD
'Splendor'
Ruling Angelic Intelligence:
Michael

NETZACH
'Victory'
Ruling Angelic Intelligence:
Haniel

YESOD
'Foundation'
Ruling Angelic Intelligence:
Gabriel

MALKUTH
'Kingdom'
Ruling Angelic Intelligence:
Sandalphon

> *"I made it beautiful with the multitude of its branches, and all the trees of Eden, which were in the garden of God, were jealous of it."* ~ Ezekiel 31:9

These Sephira are the emanations of creation beginning with Kether *(the crown)*, and working on down to Malkuth *(the kingdom)* through the path of the holy lightning bolt. However, there are only ten stations on the tree, the eleventh Sephira is known as a Non-Sephira, and its name is *'Da'ath'*. Da'ath it is the gateway into the realm of the Sitra Ahra, home of The Tree of Death. It exists *'in-between'* the two trees.

As the Tree of Life, the Tree of Death is comprised of ten Qliphothic spheres or husks, each with their own attributes and intelligences. They are the *'backside'* of the ten Sephira and thus, share attributes. MacGregor Mathers describes them,

> *"The Qliphoth, Qelippot or Klippot are "the representation of evil or impure spiritual forces in Jewish mysticism."*

Like their counterpart the Sephira, they are laid out as follows,

~ Thaumiel: *'Duality Of God'*

Rulling Demonic Intelligence: *Satan And Moloch*

~ Ghogiel: *'The Hinders'*

Rulling Demonic Intelligence: *Beelzebub*

~ Satariel: *'The Concealers'*

Rulling Demonic Intelligence: *Lucifuge*

~ Agshekeloh: *'The Breakers In Pieces'*

Rulling Demonic Intelligence: *Astaroth*

~ Golohab: *'The Burners'*

Rulling Demonic Intelligence: *Asmodeus*

~ Tagiriron: *'The Disputers'*

Rulling Demonic Intelligence: *Belphegor*

~ Herab Serapel: *'Ravens Of The Burning God'*

Rulling Demonic Intelligence: *Baal/Bael*

~ Samael: *'Poison Of God'*

Rulling Demonic Intelligence: *Adrammelek*

~ Gamaliel: *'The Obscene Ones'*

Rulling Demonic Intelligence: *Lilith*

~ Lilith: *'The Whisperers'*

Rulling Demonic Intelligence: Naahema

The Tree Of Death

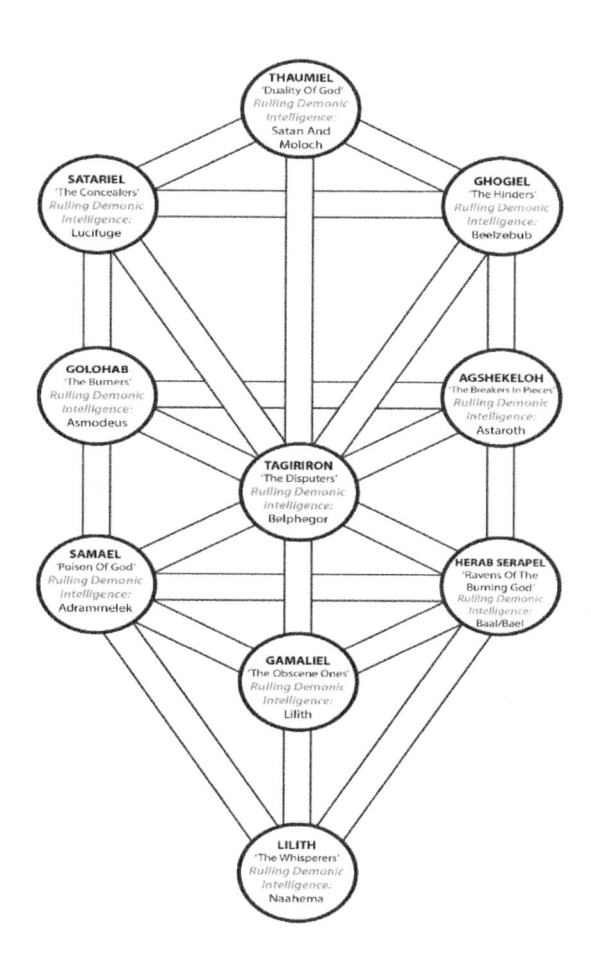

THAUMIEL
'Duality Of God'
Rulling Demonic Intelligence:
Satan And Moloch

SATARIEL
'The Concealers'
Rulling Demonic Intelligence:
Lucifuge

GHOGIEL
'The Hinders'
Rulling Demonic Intelligence:
Beelzebub

GOLOHAB
'The Burners'
Rulling Demonic Intelligence:
Asmodeus

AGSHEKELOH
'The Breakers In Pieces'
Rulling Demonic Intelligence:
Astaroth

TAGIRIRON
'The Disputers'
Rulling Demonic Intelligence:
Belphegor

SAMAEL
'Poison Of God'
Rulling Demonic Intelligence:
Adrammelek

HERAB SERAPEL
'Ravens Of The Burning God'
Rulling Demonic Intelligence:
Baal/Bael

GAMALIEL
'The Obscene Ones'
Rulling Demonic Intelligence:
Lilith

LILITH
'The Whisperers'
Rulling Demonic Intelligence:
Naahema

Ravens

A Poison Tree

"I was angry with my friend:
I told my wrath, my wrath did end.
I was angry with my foe:
I told it not, my wrath did grow.

And I watered it in fears,
Night and morning with my tears;
And I sunned it with smiles,
And with soft deceitful wiles.

And it grew both day and night,
Till it bore an apple bright;
And my foe beheld it shine,
And he knew that it was mine.

And into my garden stole,

When the night had veil'd the pole:

In the morning glad I see,

My foe outstretched beneath the tree."

~ *William Blake*

Within this grimoire, the Qliphoth *'A'arab Zaraq' (Hebrew AaRB TzRQ)* translated as *'Ravens of Dispersion'*, will be worked with. This Qliphoth is also known as Harab Serapel, translated as *'Ravens of the Burning God'*. I will be referring to this Qliphothic Sphere by both titles throughout this work. I believe the title Harab Serapel and its description fully encompass the fiery Intent of the black magician in the role of *'The Burning God'* accessing the immense power of the demonic *'Ravens of Dispersion'*. To understand this Qliphothic sphere more, we must first examine the qualities of its reverse or mirrored/reflected side, the Sephirah *'Netzach'*.

Netzach is Eternity, it encompasses the attributes of endurance, victory and perseverance but most importantly Intent. It channels *'Severity'* from Gevurah, and must be balanced by Hod, *'Splender'*, as to not loose complete control. Hod is control and restraint, while Netzach is force and unrestrained drive. Both of these Sephira are balanced within Yesod, *'Foundation'*, essentially creating controlled drive. The controlled force that is essential for successful growth and ascent. Netzach is pure Intent needed to overcome any, and all obstacles. Though if it is not balanced it becomes unrestrained lust, selfishness and desire.

Contrary to popular belief, the Qliphothic Spheres do not have opposite attributes of their counterpart Sephirah, but instead have a contrary goal. As an example, Netzach is pure drive balanced by restraint, while Harab Serapel is also pure drive, but unrestrained. As well, Netzach is driven to establish Order, while Harab Serapel is driven to establish nothing but its own Intent. Harab Serapel is not influenced by the restraint of Hod, but by the Qlipa Samael, *'The Poison Of God',* and so thus is pure drive infused with poisoned severity. As well, just as Netzach Channels Gevurah, *'Severity'*, Harab Serapel channels

Golohab, *'The Burners'*. Gevurah is authority and strength without mercy, and this trait is reflected in Golohab and infused into Harab Serapel. However, Gevurah is severity in order and control, while Golohab is severity that destroys that control.

This grimoire is designed to concentrate on accessing the unstoppable force that exists within Harab Serapel, so as to overcome any obstacle that may stand in one's way. However, one cannot simply pick up this grimoire and fully access this Qliphothic sphere without first being fully Intent on obtaining what it is that is truly needed. One's Intent cannot be in question, and hesitation must not hold one back or have sway on the black magician. To utilize this grimoire one must be driven. They must want their desired end so bad that they will stop at nothing to obtain it. They must already be running at full speed to jump onto the barreling freight train that Harab Serapel is, or be crushed beneath it. This is the base nature and power of Harab Serapel. It is within this energetic current that you will access this Qliphothic sphere and become joined with unimaginable and unstoppable power and strength.

Access to this Qlipha is dependent upon raw emotional energy, emotion that cannot be faked or reenacted. Emotion that runs deep within, and is born of frustration and anger. This grimoire is for one who has tried all roads and avenues, and been blocked. It is in this moment of *'The Last Resort'*, the moment of the *'All or Nothing'* & *'Do or Die'*, that this grimoire is accessed, this Qliphothic sphere tapped into. One has no friends, family or allies in this battle. All there is, is self and getting what is needed at all costs. No one or thing will stand in the black magician's way. They will go through friends and family if they try and stop the magician from reaching their goal. Nothing will slow the magician down. Everyone and everything is expendable, as long as the magician obtains their desired end. There is no control here, no restraint. This is extremism at its finest. This is raw, basic, instinctual…*primal*. The Demons of Harab Serapel are known as the *"Ravens of the Burning God who reject even their own"*. This description shows the ruthlessness in the pursuit self-interest.

I have decided to utilize the Solomonic magical tradition in this grimoire, by way of applying magical seals, pentacles and methods stemming from the Greater and Lesser Keys of Solomon. However, these have been *'updated'* and reverse engineered, for the purpose of this work with a Chaos Magic sub-text. I have chosen to utilize the base magical systems of the Greater and Lesser Keys of Solomon because of their close ties to Judaic magic and philosophy, which of course include The Trees of Life and Death. As well, several demons *(including Bael which is worked with in this grimoire)* associated with The Tree of Death are listed within the Lesser Key and worked with, thus making this an obvious resource to connect to and draw from. However, as stated, there is an element of Chaos Magic that underlies and is woven through this system. These elements are incorporated to draw out the most potent parts of Solomonic magic when working with the Qliphoth, from a Left Hand Path perspective.

This grimoire is for the black magician who will let nothing stand in their way. They are the center of the universe, all moves according to their will. No one, No Thing, No Spirit, No God, Will Stop Them. When the unstoppable and tremendous force of Harab Serapel is infused into the black magician, the universe itself kneels before them…

The Mask Of Arab Zaraq

Into The Sitra Ahra

"...and if you gaze into the abyss, the abyss gazes also into you." ~ *Neitzsche*

To work with the energies and intelligences of the Qliphoth, the black magician must first access them. The technique that is presented here is very unique and powerful. With ritual, the circle and triangle of arte act as the vehicle wherein the black magician raises power, makes spirit contact and causes change within the Consensual Reality Matrix. Herein is presented a similar form of operation. As stated earlier in this work, elements of the Greater and Lesser Keys of Solomon will be utilized within this grimoire, for reasons already given. That being said, the First Pentacle of the Moon *(fig. 49 in the Greater Key of Solomon)*, is implemented into this magical system as *'The Doorway'* into the Sitra Ahra. Concerning this, within the

Greater Key of Solomon, the *'Editor's Note'* states;

"The Pentacle (fig. 49) is a species of hieroglyphic representation of a door or gate. In the center is written the Name IHVH. On the right hand are the Names IHV, IHVH, AL, and IHH. On the left hand are the names of the Angels: Schioel, Vaol, Yashiel, and Vehiel. The versicle above the Names on either side is from Psalm cvii. 16:- -'He hath broken the Gates of brass, and- smitten the bars of iron in sunder."

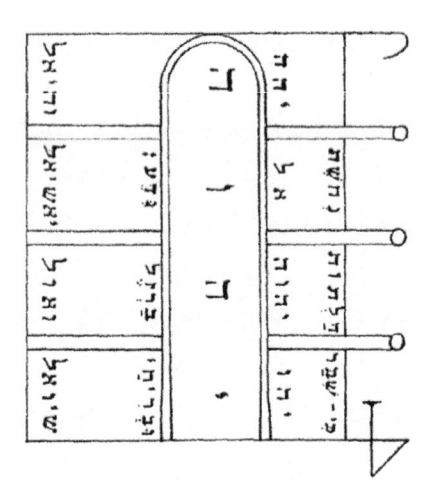

Of all the pentacles presented within the Greater Key, this is the only one which is truly unique and exhibits a strange occult usage that eludes to ceremonial practice. It is out of place when in comparison to the other pentacles, and meant to stand out or be noticed. Within the design, holy sacred names of the Hebrew God and angels are found, giving license and protection to the magician making the journey. From the editor's note,

"The versicle above the Names on either side is from Psalm cvii. 16:- -'He hath broken the Gates of brass, and- smitten the bars of iron in sunder."

We can see this is clearly a vehicle that no barrier can restrict, though this phrase isn't magical in nature per say, but descriptive. It provides description of the vehicles use. This design is obviously intended to be utilized in a practical way as a vehicle that transcends dimensions of time and space.

It is also interesting to note here that the idea of creating a doorway to travel to other dimensional spaces is not confined to the Greater Key. Contained within *"The Book of Shades"* circa 10th century C.E., published by Corvus Books and edited by E.A. St. George, is a rite that describes creating a secret doorway on a cave wall or floor, for travel into other realms,

"Thou shalt make a secret gateway within a place where no other man may come, like to a cave which others know not. There shalt thou mark out a doorway into the earth. Thou alone shall polish the doorway in the rock until it is smooth. And the door shall be marked with all the names of Allah, ere it is opened, lest evil forces come forth from the earth's heart to invade the world of men. And when the door is made, thou shalt remain within the cave, fasting and praying and burning incense. Thou shalt burn the incense and call upon the angels to protect thee. For in the time when Alnitak is high in the heavens, then the door shall seem to open and thy spirit shall move where it will within the earth." As well, within the Simon *"Necronomicon"*, we also find this magical doorway being utilized.

Said to be Chaldean in origin, it is known as The First Gate of NANNA *(The Moon)*, called SIN. Interestingly, the Necronomicon, The Book of Shades and the Greater Key, all utilize the same esoteric doorway design, insert the names of their gods and spirts within that design, and attribute the portals operation to the time of the waxing crescent moon *(as seen pictured)*, or at least at night when the moon is present.

However, the concept of interdimensional portals being drawn or carved out of the land is not limited to rites in literature, but exists in actual physical example,

"A huge mysterious door-like structure has recently been discovered in the Hayu Marca mountain region of Southern Peru. Hayu Marca, 35 kilometers from the city of Puno has long been revered by local Indians as the "City of the Gods"..." The door, or the 'Puerta de Hayu Marca' (Gate of the gods/spirits) has been at some time in the distant past carved out of a natural rock face and in all measures exactly seven meters in height by seven meters in width with a smaller alcove in the center at the base, which measures in at just under two meters in height"..." It turned out that the native Indians of the region had a legend that spoke of 'A gateway to the lands of the gods', and in that legend, it was said that in times long past, great heroes had gone to join their gods and passed through the gate for a glorious new life of immortality, and on rare occasions

those men returned for a short time with their gods to 'inspect all the lands in the kingdom' through the gate. Another legend tells of the time when the Spanish Conquistadors arrived in Peru, and looted gold and precious stones from the Inca tribes - and one Incan priest of the temple of the seven rays named Aramu Maru fled from his temple with a sacred golden disk known as 'The key of the gods of the seven rays', and hid in the mountains of Hayu Marca. He eventually came upon the doorway which was being watched by shaman priests.

He showed them the key of the gods and a ritual was performed with the conclusion of a magical occurrence initiated by the golden disk which opened the portal, and according to the legend blue light did emanate from a tunnel inside. The priest Aramu Maru handed the golden disk to the shaman and then passed through the portal 'never to be seen again'. Archeologists have observed a small hand sized circular depression on the right hand side of the small entranceway, and have theorized that this is where a small disk could be placed and held by the rock." ~ Paul Damon, 1996

Peru is not the only site in the world to have such *'stargates'*, they are found all over the world.

Though perhaps the most significant and relevant example to this chapter, concerning the use *'gateways'* for travel into other realms, lies in a section from *"The Book of the Arab"* within *"In Search of the Nameless City"*, compiled by Bob Culp, member of The Esoteric Order of Dagon,

"So it was that the riddle of the Hand and the Key on the keystones of the outer arch and the inner portal above the gates of Irem, constituted yet another obstacle to be overcome. It is written in the Magi's Book of Frashkart that the Sigil of the Great Seal of Solomon has the power to cause the Hand to grasp the Key, and dispel the barrier to that beyond."

This is indeed a riddle to be solved, and if one can unlock its secret, they are able to travel all the dimensions of reality and everywhere *In-Between*. I can't help but believe I have solved this riddle by utilizing the Hexagram *(a seal)* of Solomon, and inserting the *Key* that is the

Doorway, into it to, *'dispel the barrier to that beyond'*. The Hand must Grasp the Key and open the Gateway.

The above-mentioned gateways transport the consciousness of the magician into *'the realms of the gods'*. However, as shown within The Greater Key, The Book of Shades and The Simon Necronomicon, different gods, spirits and *'Coordinates'* are utilized, for different desired destinations. The doorway is a vehicle waiting for the correct information to be entered. Therefore, a new gateway must be fashioned for the black magician to part the veil, and enter into the chasmic abyss of the Sitra Ahra. Like the gateways discussed, this gateway too transports the consciousness of the black magician into other realms, in this case the Qliphothic sphere/reality A'arab ~ Zaraq. This is true occult technology.

The Grand Gateway

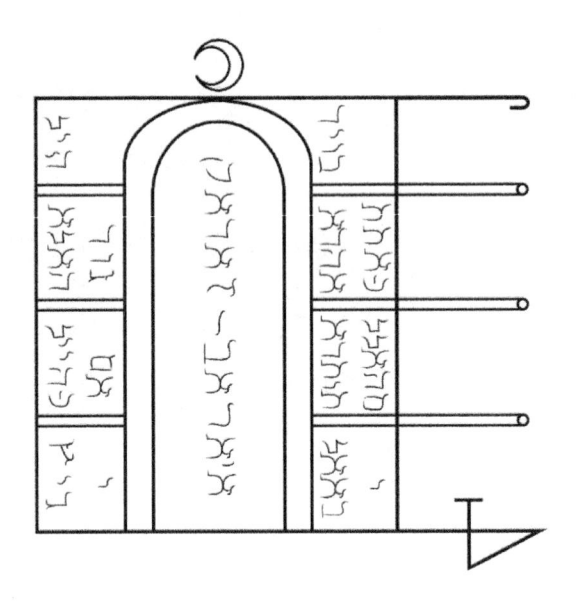

The Doorway (Close Up)

The above illustrations set the Doorway *(fig. 49)* within the Hexagram of Solomon. Though, like the doorway itself, alternate power names have been inserted. The reasoning behind this is of course, to amplify the gateway with the appropriate polarization and energies of the Sitra Ahra. This complete design is incredibly powerful and surging with energy. Having used this vehicle, I can say with certainty that it is fully operational and a vital tool for any black magician to utilize with this Qliphothic system.

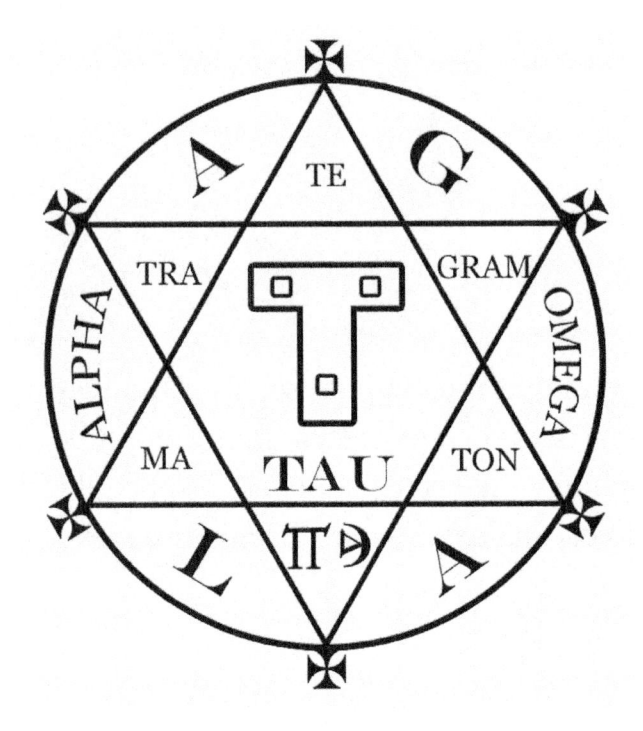

As mentioned, like the reverse engineering of the Hexagram of Solomon, the Doorway itself has been augmented with the correct names, descriptions and sigils to activate the portal into the Sitra Ahra and specifically into A'arab – Zaraq/Harab Serapel. In the center of the doorway is written in Hebrew the Name *'A'arab-Zaraq'*. On the right hand is written *'Bael'*, *'Sitra Ahra'*, *'Void'*. On the left hand is written *'Getzphiel'* and *'Halahel'*. The versicle above the words on either side state: *"I Shall Pass, I Am God"*.

The purpose of The Grand Gateway is to journey into the Sitra Ahra and Qlipha, to experience them in spirit and consciousness, before working with them in ritual on the physical plane.

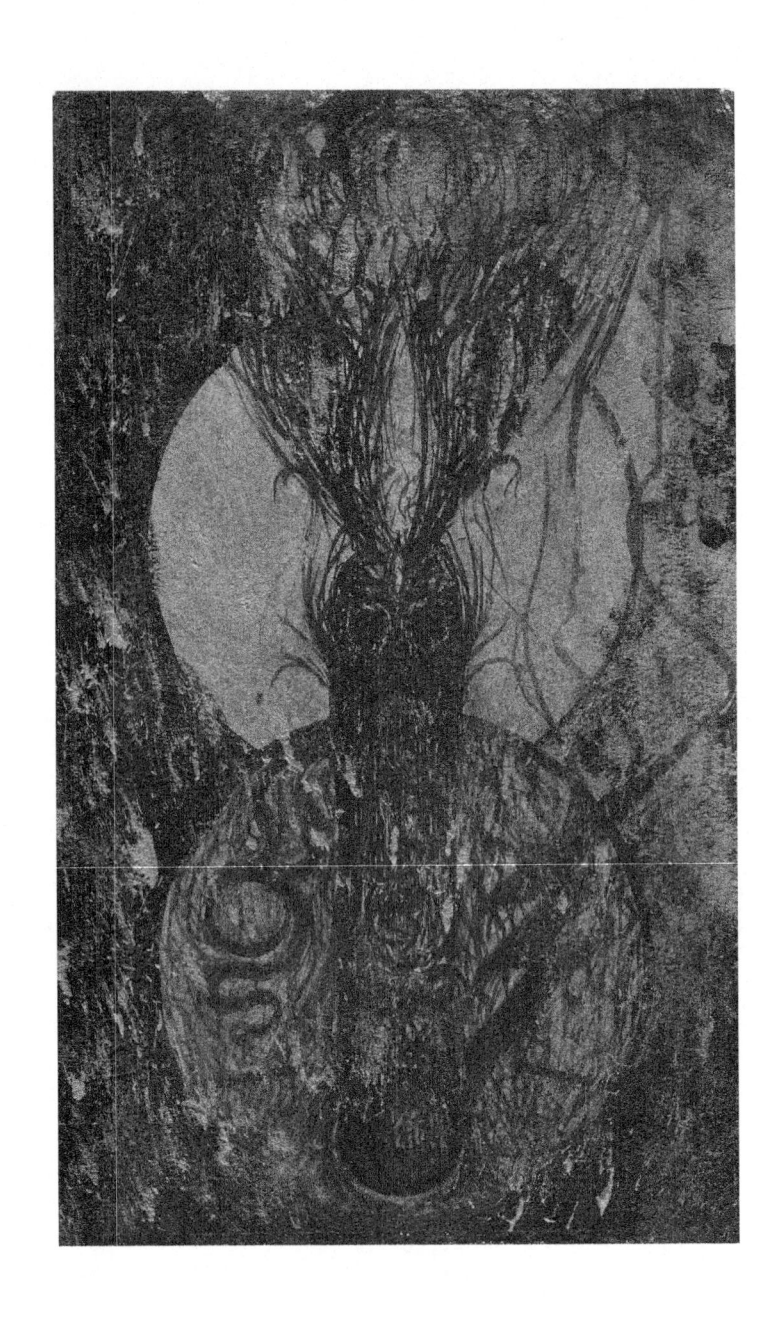

Venus Illigitima

The Rite Of The Grand Gateway

Begin by securing a location where you will not be disturbed, this can be either inside a temple, or out beneath the stars. Either way it truly does not matter, as you are not interacting with entities on this plane of existence, but traveling into another where contact is established. The location must be safe, in a place that no animal or human can cross paths with, as the black magician may not be totally aware of their surroundings when in rite and needs to be secure. That being said, the location of the doorway is not important as long as it can be opened.

The diameter of The Grand Gateway is 14ft, quite large for a circle, however, as stated, this is not a traditional magical circle, but a vehicle into the neither realms. Obviously, The Grand Gateway and Doorway can have new coordinates plugged in to get to as many destinations as one can imagine. The black magician should immediately be able to see how useful this tool is, and the applications that can be applied to it.

One can use many different materials to create The Grand Gateway, salt, flour, paint, etc. However, it should be as exact as possible. To do this, measuring is advisable. Creating The Grand Gateway will take time, the black magician should make sure to mind their thoughts, that they stay focused on the rite and all it involves, rather than on mundane affairs. Once created, light and place large black candles within the small triangles surrounding The Grand Gateway. When all has been set in place, rest by sitting in the Doorway and meditating. Let your thoughts wander, don't try and control them. See what images come through. Even though The Grand Gateway hasn't been activated yet, it is still very powerful and ready to be opened. On the other side of the Doorway/seal lies A'arab ~ Zaraq, so energies will definitely be felt and picked up.

When rested, begin the rite by laying in the Doorway, arms laid flat on the ground at your sides. Relax and take several long slow breaths. You should immediately feel the energy matrix that surrounds and runs through you. It feels like a light electric current running through your body, making your fingertips tingle. As well, it is natural to feel a little anxiety, as this rite is intense and deals with very dark currents. Visualize the circle and doorway you are laying in, as if you were floating above yourself, looking down at your body and The Grand Gateway. Visualize the ground drop away behind you, leaving you and The Grand Gateway suspended above The Great Void.

The Void is Da'ath, a Non – Qliphoth which will be discussed in detail, in its own forthcoming volume. Within the Void dwells the dark entity known as Choronzon. Choronzon is the Gate Keeper of the Sitra Ahra. Many black magicians have tried to cross The Void and failed. They donned their armor and went to war with Choronzon, only to be torn asunder. One does not *'fight'* Choronzon, there is no chance to be the victor. One submits to Choronzon and is devoured,

"The Vaults of Zin exist, they lie within the greyscale twilight of the heart and mind, just outside of vision, where the spirit sometimes

wanders in the dead of night. Some willingly travel there 'in search of', while others discover the nightmare they dwell in, horrified and seeking escape. Regardless of intention, The Vaults (The Void) draw one down, as quicksand consumes and absorbs its helpless victim. Some helplessly fight against the sinking, while other stand silent, allowing themselves to be devoured as if by an enormous black serpent swallowing its prey whole." ~ *'The Black Book of Azathoth'*

The black magician must vibrate the energies and sacred names of this Qlipha. Choronzon must also be summoned as the Gatekeeper, to pass through the Doorway to the other side. When laying within the Doorway of The Grand Gateway, suspended over the great black chasm of The Void, one must begin to slowly, softly chant,

"BA'EL ~ A'ARAB ~ ZARAQ,

CHORONZON,

HARAB ~ ZARAQ,

Open The Gates,

BA'EL ~ A'ARAB ~ ZARAQ,

HARAB ~ SERAPEL,

HARAB ~ ZARAQ,

I Shall Pass,

BA'EL ~ A'ARAB ~ ZARAQ,

GETZPHIEL,

HARAB ~ ZARAQ,

I Am God"

Repeat this mantra/chant/call over and over. As you chant build in vibration and volume, visualize a great and massive black snake slowly, so slowly winding its way *'up'* to you from behind, from within the great darkness of The Void. Those who suffer from thalassophobia *(the fear of the ocean and what lies within)* will find it difficult to perform this rite, especially since one is summoning this great sinister force, from behind, unable to see it. It is akin to laying face up on the surface of the ocean, and calling up Leviathan from the great black depths to devour you.

Feel Choronzon's sinister presence, just as feeling one stand right behind you, breathing over your shoulder. As Choronzon slithers and slowly glides *'up'* to you, visualize the great beast opening its jaws. It pauses, then in one sudden movement strikes and takes you down within itself...Once *'consumed'*, the black magician gains entrance into the Sitra Ahra and specifically A'arab ~ Zaraq.

Corridors Of Niantiel

Getzphiel: The Burning God

"...Every night I burn,
Every night I fall again,
Every night I burn,
Scream the animal scream,
Every night I burn,
Dream the crow black dream,
Dream the crow black dream."
~ The Cure, *'Burn'*

Within these workings, the black magician dons the role and position of *'The Burning God'*. As stated, Harab Serapel translates as, *'Ravens Of The Burning God'*. This title rightfully suggests that there are two parties involved; one, the *'Ravens Of Dispersion'*, and secondly, *'The Burning God'*. At the core of Harab Serapel lies a demon by the name, *Getzphiel* which is as a volcano of raw fiery force. Raging with an intensity that is unmatched, Getzphiel is the life blood of Harab Serapel, its foundation. Getzphiel is the engine that powers A'arab Zaraq.

However, the title, *'The Burning God'* also aptly applies to the sharp Intent, the black magician embodies in spirit and mind when working with this Qliphothic sphere. The black magician *'Burns'* with fiery desire that has no end, and acts as *'God'* of his universe. Therefore, by *invoking* Getzphiel, the black magician becomes, *'The Burning God'*. Invoking such a powerful force within, can only be done for short periods of time, as the human vessel cannot contain the intense raw power of Getzphiel for long periods without suffering in some way.

Little to nothing has been written or recorded of Getzphiel, save for his name and general existence. Therefore, as with many of the inhabitants of the Qliphoth, the only way to get to understand them and their essence, was to either evoke or invoke them, and record my own personal experiences. With Getzphiel, I knew it was a force to bring inside of myself, to commune and be one with.

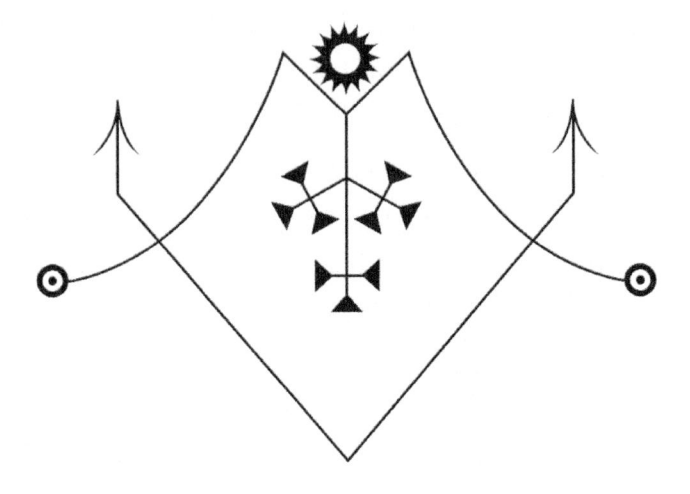

The Invocation Of Getzphiel

Begin this rite by laying out the sigil of Getzphiel in place of where the triangle of arte would be, in relation to the magic circle of course. Light several red candles for light, placement isn't important. Sit in the magic circle and gaze at Getzphiel's sigil. Visualize a red searing heat or energy emanating from it, see it burning. When ready, begin the invocation, and as it is said, visualize the flames of Getzphiel's sigil flowing into your solar plexus, filling you. Call,

"Blazing Spirit Of Unending Might,

I Call You Forth,

~ G ~ E ~ T ~ Z ~ P ~ H ~ I ~ E ~ L ~

Demon Of Fire And Brimstone,

Incinerator Of Weakness,

Purifier Of Intent,

Hear My Words, See My Signs!

Come Forth Before Me Great One,

~ G ~ E ~ T ~ Z ~ P ~ H ~ I ~ E ~ L ~

I Open Myself Unto You...

Join With Me,

Ignite My Essence With Your Scorching Drive!

Be As One With Me,

I Invite You In,

Take Hold Of My Essence,

Push Me Beyond My Restraints,

Beyond My Mortal Limitations,

Raise Me Up Upon Your Burning Pylon,

*So I May Pass Through The Searing Flames
Of Purity,*

So I May Become Unstoppable In My Intent,

~ G ~ E ~ T ~ Z ~ P ~ H ~ I ~ E ~ L ~

Be One With Me…

Die Zersetzer

The Ravens Of Dispersion

"...His eyes have all the seeing of a demon's that is dreaming..."

~ Edgar Allen Poe, 'The Raven'

The Ravens Of Dispersion *(or of Death)*, are the demonic inhabitants of the Qliphothic sphere *'A'arab Zaraq'*. They take the form of giant ravenous black ravens with burning red eyes, and are described as breaking forth from the depths of a blazing volcano. These fiery dwellers of this Qliphothic sphere have several titles and spellings of their name:

A'arab Zaraq, *(A'arab Tzereq, Ghoreb Zereq)*:

'Ravens of Dispersion'

Hebrew: AaRB-TzRQ

And

<u>Harab Serapel</u>:

'Ravens of the Burning God'

<u>Hebrew</u>: HRB-SRRAL

These demonic intelligences are uncontrolled and unstoppable. They move with a grace and speed unmatched by most other entities, oftentimes being experienced as a swarm or black blurs. When calling them forth, the Black Magician does not call upon one, but the entire *'Unkindness', (group of ravens)*. Though they are willing to turn on their own to achieve their personal desires, they are called upon as one uncontrolled swarm. However that being said, there are times when only one appears and represents the entire Unkindness.

When working with the Unkindness, obviously one does not command them to do one's will, as they cannot be controlled. In this sense, they are as the *Taw-All* of the Djinn written of in *"The Book Of Smokeless Fire"*, they cannot be commanded, but work to achieve a common goal with the black magician; destroying obstacles. The Unkindness is just that, unkind. They have no remorse for their actions, no sympathy for those who fall in their wake. In a sense this state of being is truly Satanic, as here the self, one's desires and fulfilling those desires are all that matter, and nothing else. Pure selfish indulgence without fear of emotional repercussion.

Although the Unkindness is known for its unstoppable force, it is also known for *Death*. As stated, any and all who stand in the way of the desired end, fall to the wayside, and many do not survive. It is said that a Raven of Death assisted Qayin in the burial of Abel,

> *"Some traditions state that after the murder (of Abel) was committed, Qayin was guided by a black raven (A'arab Zaraq – the Raven of Dispersion and Death) to dig a grave, into*

which He sowed the corpse of His weak brother Abel, thus the First Harvester and Killer also became the First Gravedigger and Lord of the First Grave Mound (the First Gulgalta)." ~ N.A-A. 218, 'Liber Falxifer'

The connection the Unkindness shares with death is quite evident and should not be overlooked, as the Black Magician can utilize and tap into this intense force when performing necromantic rites.

Seen a totem that walks between the worlds, the Raven has access to hidden gnosis. They are living oracles into the occult realm of the unseen. There is an old Irish proverb,

"To have a raven's knowledge"

which means to have a seer's supernatural powers. It is said in the Hebrides *(islands off the coast of Scotland)*, that by using a raven's skull to give a newborn its first drink, the child will be infused with gifts of prophecy and wisdom.

The Ravens of Dispersion share all of the traits assigned to the earthly raven, they are nearly interchangeable, a reflection. Seeing a raven is akin to seeing a unicorn or gryphon, they are spiritual magic and mystery embodied into material form. The Unkindness of Harab Serapel, appearing as a single solid raven to Qayin and Noah, shows that like the fallen angels that came to earth and *'fashioned'* for themselves material bodies, to *'experience'* the daughters of man, so too are the ravens of A'arab Zaraq able to take on a solid material form within this plane of existence.

Not only are the Ravens of Dispersion seen as having strong connections with death and the dead, prophecy, and forceful Intent, but they also embody the spirit of Rebellion,

"When Noah sent the raven to see whether the waters were abated, it refused to go, saying: "Thy Lord hateth me; for, while seven of other species were received into the ark, only two of mine were admitted. And thou also hatest me; for, instead of sending one from the sevens, thou sendest me! If I am met by the angel of heat or by the angel of cold, my species will be lost." Noah answered the raven: "The world hath no need of thee; for thou art good

neither for food nor for sacrifice." ~ Sanh. 108b; Gen. R. xxxiii. 6

This sentiment is echoed in the poem *'Noah's Raven'*,

> *"Why should I have returned?*
> *My knowledge would not fit into theirs.*
> *I found untouched the desert of the unknown,*
> *Big enough for my feet. It is my home.*
> *It is always beyond them. The future*
> *Splits the present with the echo of my voice.*
> *Hoarse with fulfillment, I never made promises." ~ W.S. Merwin*

Eventually the raven did go, but it never returned to Noah. In this rebellion against Noah, we see a strong likeness and connection to the rebellion Qayin set against YHVH,

> *"Then Cain went away from the presence of the LORD and settled in the land of Nod, east of Eden." ~ Genesis 4:16-17*

And rightfully so, as both YHVH and Noah cast these beings aside without a second thought, in sight of their own personal pursuits. This is true irony, as Noah and

YHVH both accessed the selfish adverse strength and qualities within the Qliphothic sphere of A'arab Zaraq to accomplish their own goals, which spur from qualities associated with the Tree of Life; harmonic control. They turned on their own. Not only is the Unkindness in connection to Qayin shown here, but also within Qayin's descendant, *'Tubal Qayin'* (תובל קין). Tubal Qayin was known for his expert metal working skills, but also for forging weapons of war and murder. Rashi *(medieval rabbi and author)* speculates that Tubal Qayin translates loosely as one who,

> "Spiced and refined Cain's craft to make weapons for murderers."

Weapons are used to destroy any and all opposition that exists on one's path. In this way, the connection with A'arab Zaraq is made.

A'arab Zaraq, *'The Ravens of Dispersion'*, Harab Serapel, *'The Ravens of the Burning God',* both adequate in title and description. For this force, this *Unkindness,* is unharnessed devastation. Prophecy shines in the eyes of those who would leave death in their wake. And the eyes of these demonic ravens, blaze as an inferno of everlasting Hellfire.

Harab Serapel

The Rite Of The Ravenous Ravens

"The dead are lying in the fields,
Oh, hear Her Kraaak and cry!
The gaping wounds, a raven's yield,
She comes hungry from the sky."

~ S. Black, "The Morigan"

Sigil Of The Raven

This rite is designed to forcibly remove all obstacles preventing ascent in one's life. It is akin to unlocking all locked doors or unblocking all blocked paths of opportunity in one's life. There are times in one's life where they feel no matter what they try to accomplish, it ends in disaster or failure. Whichever path they try to traverse, is blocked by some obstacle, whether it be physical or situational.

This rite is designed to access the unstoppable force of the Unkindness, and apply it to removing any and all *(people or situations)* that stand in the black magician's way forward. Though as stated in the Introduction, one must already possess the fiery Intent needed, and have invoked Getzphiel before going forth with this rite. The invocation of Getzphiel doesn't need to be performed right before this rite, just sometime in the recent past.

This rite does not gently remove the black magician's obstacles, it annihilates them. It unleashes the Unkindness to swarm and ravenously consume whatever lies in the black magician's path, that wises to deter them. One initially thinks that this is all fine and good, but deep thought is required on this act before performing it, as the power unleashed is so devastating.

Within this system, bloodletting is utilized. This is natural in workings with the Qliphoth. BA'EL ~ A'ARAB ~ ZARAQ presides over this Qlipha, and requires blood as sacrifice for His assistance. More so, this sphere is associated with the Qanaanite path which worshiped BAAL, and of course stems from Qayin and Tubal Qayin, wielder of waring weapons and bloodshed. Blood is strong on this path. Blood is the life essence of the black magician, it is the soul signature. One's very essence flows through the blood. Therefore, it is a fitting sacrifice to offer one's soul essence to these dark spirits within this current.

The Rite

Begin by laying out the Sigil of the Raven in place of where the traditional triangle of arte would be, of course in association with a magical circle. This working can be performed outside or in, as long as one is not disturbed. Ignite several black candles for light, placement isn't important. On a side note, purple is also a powerful color for candles etc. in Qliphothic rites. Once everything is laid out, take a moment and meditate in the magical circle, gazing at the Sigil of the Raven. Take in the importance of this rite, it isn't just another magical working, this rite is infused with a drive that is unmatched. This rite will violently change one's life, and most likely affect those in the life of the black magician, possibly in a negative fashion. This rite ensures the black magician get what they want, regardless of who suffers for it. Though this is something to consider, the black magician should also contemplate what they will obtain in their life because of the working. Once done, focus on the Sigil of the Raven, and begin the evocation,

"I Call Out To, And Into The Realm Of The Sitra Ahra,

Into The Twilight Of The In-Between Spaces,

Into The Realm Of Aching Shadow,

A'ARAB ~ ZARAQ,

Hear My Words, See My Signs,

I Call To You In Strength And Power,

Hear My Voice Echo Throughout The Negative Lands,

As A Wind Travels Vast And Wide,

Hear My Call,

HARAB ~ SERAPEL

I Call You Forth Into This Temple. X3

~

Ravens Of The Burning God,

Ravens Of Strength And Shadow,

I Call You Forth To Join With Me,

Ravens Of Dispersion,

Hear Me On This Hallowed Night. X3

~

Go Forth From This Temple With Fiery Might,

Remove All Obstacles In Way Of My Ascent,

As A Flaming Arrow, My Way Forward Must Be Cleared!

Unkindness I Call Upon You All,

Go Forth And Feed Upon Those Who Would Stand In My Way,

Tear Apart All Who Would Resist Me,

Lay To Waste Any Who Would Refuse Me,

Bring Them To Their Knees. X3

~

Unkindness, I Offer You My Blood As Sacrifice,

Drink In My Essence And Strength,

The Unholy Spirit Getzphiel Flows Through Me,

~

The Burning God Is Within Me, For I Am He And He Is Me,

Join In This Unholy Communion Before The Ever Watchful Eyes Of BA'EL ~ A'ARAB ~ ZARAQ,

HARAB ~ SERAPEL,

A'ARAB ~ ZARAQ,

Go Forth... X3

Once the evocation and sacrifice has been done, the rite is finished. Now that the Unkindness has been unleashed, there is nothing that can negate its Intent and strength. Be ready.

Baal

The Ravens Of Devouring Death

". . . craving for carrion, the dark raven shall have its say, and tell the eagle how it fared at the feast, when, competing with the wolf, it laid bare the bones of corpses." ~ Beowulf

Sigil Of The Raven

This rite is very similar to the previous rite, though The Ravens of Dispersion are directed at a specific target, rather than a life path. This rite is designed to annihilate an enemy and all they stand for. That description is left up to interpretation. Like the previous rite, begin by laying out the Sigil of the Raven in place of where the traditional triangle of arte would be, of course in association with a magical circle. This working can be performed outside or in, as long as one is not disturbed. Ignite several black candles for light, placement isn't important. Once everything is laid out, take a moment and meditate in the magical circle, gazing at the Sigil of the Raven. When ready call,

"*Blackness hear me…*

I call into the gulf of the darkest abyss,

Across the frozen windswept fields…

A'arab-Zaraq…

Come forth…

~

Ravens of Death…

Hear my words of devotion,

See my signs of sacrifice upon the land,

I call you forth into this temple of shades.

~

Harab-Serapel…

Use your sharp eyes to see my enemy,

Seek them out…

~

Use your sharp talons to fasten my enemy,

Overpower them,

Use your sharp beak to pierce my enemy,

Feast upon them…

~

Ravens of the Burning God,

Hear my call to take down my enemy,

Tear them asunder,

Shred their flesh,

Devour their soul,

Leave Nothing…

~

Unkindness…

Spirits of old,

Fly forth…

Ba'el-A'arab-Zaraq

Ba'el-A'arab-Zaraq;
King Of Hell, Lord Of Darkness

"And so, I've crawled through the eye of a needle,

Just looking for holy ground,

I've come this far for the silent grace of god,

And nothing is what I've found…

Nothing is what I found…" ~ S. Ben Qayin

Once an angel, now fallen, Bael is the ruling demon of the Qliphothic sphere A'arab Zaraq. There are several different spellings of his name such as, *'Bel'*, *'Baal'*, *'Ba'al'*, *'Ba'el'*, *'Bail'*, *'Baall'* and Hebrew: בעל. *"The Lesser Key of Solomon"* describes him,

"The first Principal Spirit is a King ruling in the East, called Bael. He maketh thee to go Invisible. He ruleth over 66 Legions of Infernal Spirits. He appeareth in divers shapes, sometimes like a Cat, sometimes like a

Toad, and sometimes like a Man, and sometimes all these forms at once. He speaketh hoarsely. This is his character which is used to be worn as a Lamen before him who calleth him forth, or else he will not do thee homage."

Bael, has taken on many forms and attributes over the centuries, as with other ancient deities *(such as Hekate)*, he has many faces. This is also reflected within the current 218 and the different faces and titles of Qayin. Bael/Ba'al has been known as Baal-Peor, Baal-Berith, Baal-Chanan and Baal-Hammon among others. Within this grimoire, the face of Bael that will be worked with is *'Ba'el-A'arab-Zaraq'*, obviously associating Bael with the Qliphothic sphere and the Ravens of Dispersion.

Bael has been worshiped in many different ways throughout time and region, though the rites associated with him all share the same primal sexuality and sacrifice, blood-letting and sex.

"...the kings of Judah had ordained to burn incense in the high places in the cities of Judah, and in the places round about Jerusalem; them also that burned incense unto Baal, to the sun, and to the moon, and to the planets, and to all the host of heaven." ~ 2 Kings 23:5

"(they) have built the high places of Baal to burn their sons in the fire as burnt offerings to Baal..." ~ Jeremiah 19:5

There is also mention of child sacrifice in, *"The Lost Book of King Og", (once said to be part of the apocryphal "Book of Giants") "originally transcribed during a several hundred year swath in and around 1400 BCE".*

Though the authenticity of this work is still in question, it does indeed seem this text is genuine. Within the work, Ba'al is a major influence and subject of discussion,

> *"Nimrod's* Nephilim *kingdom and that Rephaim land of Og sacrificed [all. . .] smaller self [children] with [effectual] [fervent] ritual,* being of one mind and spirit bleeding for Baal *to [undo] the Unspoken Mistake."* ~ *1:31*

Within the book, Ba'al is described as a strong and vicious spirit of war and malice, but also of prosperity, bestowing gifts upon his followers who offer blood sacrifice in his honor,

> *"How [in his stupidity]. . .[half-loined] Nimrod defied Baal. Thus causing Baal of the earth to guide my [unforgiving hands of war] to his death."* ~ *1:16*

The following are said to be the words of Ba'al himself, as received by a devout prophetess,

> *"I am Baal your God who delivered you from Nimrod in the Hundred Thousand Giant War.*
>
> *I am Baal of the earth who will provide the extension to the Rephaim.*

*Because of this, you will
bleed yourself before no other gods.*

I do not honor the circumcision

*It is good for the Rephaim not to know the
smaller selves.*

*You will not cut your members
for any of the other insect-sized gods that
demand it*

*May the destruction of my enemies buried
in ... their punishment until the end of time.*

*Worship me and I Baal will extend your [. . .]
of power
and give you [. . .].*

Consider this:

*A time is coming when you will all worship
Baal Hammon*

He is coming in storm. Every eye will see him

Even those that practice circumcision

*Let the enemies tremble and
let the earth shake. The great Baal of the Rephaim
stands above the insect-sized gods.*

Filth is the land of his heritage.

*All will ascribe penance and worship
Blood sacrifice is. . .
fertility I will empower. . .*

Do not tire. Baal's power. . .

as you see the [lush country]. As your crops. . .

*As Kaour the able and Farshen the palsied
served as temple stewards,*

Speaking through the smoke from the [darkened] sacrificial fire, the worship must frenzy and gash with knives and lances.

Baal your…delivers the promised extension of Rephaim [lineage].

Proclaim the power of Baal on the fertile mountain.
Continue. . .I will extend you." ~ 'The Lost Book of King Og'

As well, Bael has been featured in many works of magic throughout the centuries including, *"De Praestigiis Daemonum"* - 1536, *"The Book of The Offices of Spirits"* - 1563, *"The Book of Oberon"* – 1577, *"The Discoverie of Witchcraft"* – 1584, *"The Magical Calendar"* - 1620, *"The Lesser Key of Solomon"* – 1641, *"Paradise Lost"* – 1667", *"Dictionneaire Infernal"* – 1818, and *"The Grand Grimoire"* – 1821.

The appearance of Bael as described within *"The Lesser Key of Solomon"* is a frightful mosaic of forms,

"He appeareth in divers shapes, sometimes like a Cat, sometimes like a Toad, and sometimes like a Man, and sometimes all these forms at once."

(Image Courtesy of Dictionneaire Infernal)

Bael appears as a man once the black magician requests and presents his sigil to him. In my personal workings with him, my perception of Bael is that of a man in his 40's neatly dressed, modern in his own right. However, it is mybelief that the demon takes on the form that best suits the reality of the black magician. One should have no expectations of appearance, allowing the spirit to manifest as is needed. So many are lost to expectations, which works against the true manifestation of the spirit within the Personal Reality Grid of the black magician.

Bael has 66 legions attributed him. In ancient Rome a legion comprised of 6,000 men, so doing the math, Bael has 396,000 demonic spirits at his command. Yet those masses serving him remain nameless, save one…*Halahel*.

Sevenfold

The Raising Of Ba'el-A'arab-Zaraq

"I am Baal of the earth who will provide

The extension to the Raphaim.

Because of this, you will

Bleed yourself before no other gods." ~ Baal

The Star of Ba'el-A'arab-Zaraq

This rite is designed to summon forth lord Ba'el-A'arab-Zaraq before the black magician. This is done so that they may access the pure energies of this mighty spirit, and build a relationship with Him in working with the Qliphoth. As with use in the Lesser Key of Solomon, the black magician must wear Ba'el-A'arab-Zaraq's amulet when summoning him,

> *"This is his character which is used to be worn as a Lamen before him who calleth him forth, or else he will not do thee homage."*

Sigils to spirits are as blood and fingerprints to humans, they are specifically unique to each. Therefore, having Ba'el-A'arab-Zaraq's Layman present at the evocation as instructed, makes perfect sense, and should not only be utilized within this system, but in others as well.

Begin this rite by laying out The Star of Ba'el-A'arab-Zaraq in a place you won't be disturbed. Ignite several black or purple candles for light, and sit within the polygon connected to The Star. The way The Star of Ba'el-A'arab-Zaraq is designed directs the energy of the spirit into the polygon of the black magician, connecting them in union. The Star can also be used in rites of invocation/possession. As well, if another polygon is added to the opposite side *(mirroring the magician's polygon, i.e. circle),* the overall design is a perfect template for two magicians to do a joint rite, even outside of this system working with the Qliphoth. Soak up the energy that is racing through you from the angles The Star of Ba'el-A'arab-Zaraq. Light incense, frankincense and myrrh works well here. When ready begin the evocation, call,

The Raising

"Ba'el of earth and blood,

I call you forth on this eve of darkness,

Ba'el of storm and war,

Hear my voice echo across the vast expanse of sky.

~

Great lord of Rephaim, hear my call upon the winds,

Come forth before me in strength and might,

Ba'el-A'arab-Zaraq.

~

Rebel of the Tyrant,

The earth trembles at your presence,

Shakes beneath my feet as a terrible thunder,

May my voice race to up reach you, oh lord of blood and death,

See my signs of sacrifice and devotion out upon the land,

Bless me with your unholy presence

~

Ba'el-A'arab-Zaraq,

Offered to you is mine own essence of spirit,

Partake of my blood that is spilt out before you,

I honor thee great lord of Earth and Sky, of Sea and Air,

I call you forth, hear my call,

~

Ba'el-A'arab-Zaraq,

Lord of Harab-Serapel,

Brother of Unkindness,

I call you forth,

I call you,

I call…"

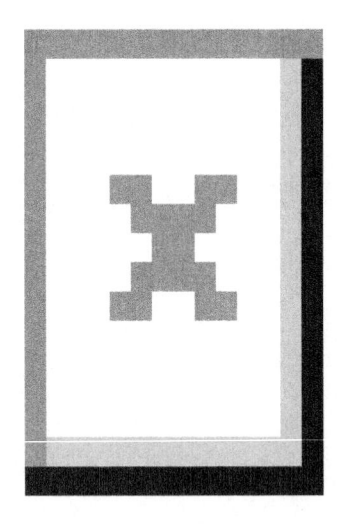

Master Of The Qliphoth

Halahel;

Unholy Darkness With The Eyes Of An Angel

*"...I threw you the obvious just to see
If there's more behind the eyes of a fallen
angel,
The eyes of a tragedy..."*

~ A Perfect Circle, '*3 Libras*'

Halahel is listed in *"The Lesser Key of Solomon"* as figure 175. Said to be a spirit that has a *'mixed nature'*, being partly *'good'* and partly *'evil'*, as the spirits in the Theurgia-Goetia, within the Lemegeton. Said to be under the rule of Ba'el, this spirit is only listed here, nowhere else can it be found, and no information given. As the spirit itself, this is both a negative and positive situation, as it is difficult to understand what preparations are needed and what experiences previous magicians have had with the spirit. However, I personally found it positive in the way that I was not influenced by description, thus giving the rite and spirit the freedom to materialize as desired, and not as expected. I always find it exciting to call upon little known or overlooked spirits in the history of magic and all its dusty tomes. Some spirits I have called forth, had not been summoned in centuries, such as the Djinn found in *"The Book of Smokeless Fire"*. I find with such spirits, that their evocation must be repeated a number of times to get a response. It is as if they are asleep or far off, roaming in the spaces of spirits. The Chaldeans believed that they had to reach the highest peaks to shout their calls to their gods. They did this because they believed their gods had created them, but then traveled on to far off spaces and forgotten them. In many of their calls. They repeatedly state to the gods to *'remember'*. They wanted them to remember their covenant, their pact of sacrifice and servitude for their Great Ones assistance. This is discussed and can be seen in the book *"Chaldean Magic"* by Lenormant. When calling upon Halahel, this should be taken into consideration.

When I called upon Halahel these are the impressions I received,

"Halahel is an old spirit, mysterious. Silent, distant. Black shadow man standing in front of a doorway/crack of blinding white light. Can't see him clearly, just silhouette. Strength emanates from him and atmosphere that surrounds the temple. Very serious spirit, no time, gets to the point."

Contact wasn't long, but intense. Halahel gives off the impression of a holy assassin, A being of few words, but strong in intent. He is willing to get his hands dirty to accomplish a goal. Of course, these are just my impressions, I encourage the black magician to perform their own evocations and experience this being *(and others)* in their own Personal Reality Grid and suspend expectation.

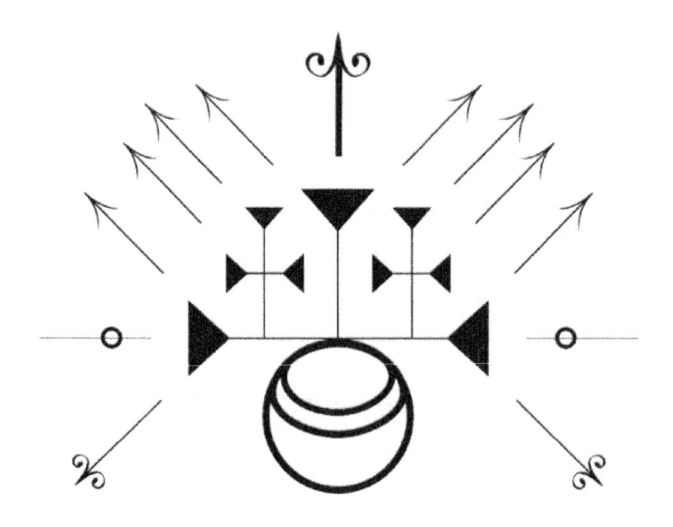

The Conjuration Of Halahel

Halahel !

I call to you from beyond the shimmering veil,

Hear my voice echo through the vast empty spaces,

Hear me great spirt of holy might,

Heavy heart, eyes alight,

Grief and rage intertwined,

As a rose plagued with thorns.

~

I call you before me Halahel,

Unholy ghost of Ba'el,

Come forth on this sacred night,

Hear me oh great spirit !

I honor you with blood and wine.

~

Brother of Ba'el,

Hear my voice soar up on high,

I call you spirit !

Open the way, spill forth your light,

I call you, hear me !

I call you !

~

Branded unholy, you walk in twilight,

Brother of angels lost,

Halahel Hear me !

Halahel I call you !

Halahel !

Venus Decomposing

Fetish Totem Of A'rab Zaraq

Through The Claws Of Eternity

Known as 'The Raven of Dispersion' or 'The Raven of Death', this shell presides over the gnosis of the Void. He is self-devouring Chaos itself. Through this knowledge, we can transmute inside the astral realms, and roam as shadows in this existential plane, which is especially useful for dream working machines, astral projections and sabbatical gatherings. The Raven as a symbol in A'rab Zaraq, symbolizes the soul of the sorcerer flying to self–liberation, leading to total ecstasy, breaking the dualities of reason and madness, life and death in an alchemical transformation in which the Sorcerer transcends Death itself, and is reborn as a strong individual becoming master of death magick and necromancy. To walk the path of A'rab Zaraq, is to walk the path of the warrior, surpassing all the obstacles on the magickal path explored. A'rabZaraq is highly connected with the magick of Lucifer, which reveals a path of pure self-illumination and transcendental gnosis.

Passing through the veils of his/her own dissolution, he became the raven of dispersion and can generate his/her own astral eggs for later workings while burning the torch of his/her own divinity. An important element to work with A'rabZaraq is to try to find the gates in dreams, so the use of a magickal mirror works very well when exploring the astral realms. The mirror can work as a catalyst of A'rab Zaraq's essence in the psychic body or the adept. Through this you can enter into utter darkness, and explore the astral tunnels which lead you to the dark side of consciousness.

To work with A'rab Zaraq, is to enter the portal of self-mastery in the art of war. Psychic skills are used to fight to transcend into the infernal light, through the broken realities and illusory masks which prevent our development in the magickal field. The invocation process of A'rab Zaraq, is the path to discover your individual skills and mastering as a warrior. It is to learn how to fight with your inner self and obstacles, and transcend reality, using your psychic abilities as weapons, and develop your occult faculties through the wisdom of the 'Formula of Putrefaction-Death-Decomposition", to emerge as a strong individual renewed and transformed. Entering the black sea of one's own capabilities and psychic developments the adept can fight and devour the eye of the black serpent that opens and devours the adept creating a self-enlightenment of his/her own magickal nature. This is a gradual process of learning diverse path workings, self-divinity mastery and self-understanding on all levels.

Baal-Qayin

The Rite Of The Black Mirror

One of the useful artifacts I found so interesting to work with, when working with A'rab Zaraq, is the magickal mirror which can be used to explore the astral realms and also to connect with other Qliphothic energies. Such artifacts work as external portals to the influx of energies from the densest of Qliphothic levels in this existential plane. The 'Shades' in mirrors can appear in a vaporous and abstract form when working properly with them. A powerful technique is to use two mirrors face to face with a small distance between them. One of the mirrors must be black backed so no light is visible through it. The second mirror, nothing is done to. The point here is to let the adept (when in trance state) visualize, and slowly start to perceive, the energies between the two mirrors.

When working with A'rab Zaraq, the idea is to draw a sigil on the black mirror, so it will act as a magickal catalyst to the ingress of such energies on that plane. First meditate until all your mental, physical and spiritual bodies become one force. Once done, you are ready to explore the essence of A'rab Zaraq. After drawing the sigil with your own blood on the black mirror, chant the following mantra during the ritual:

RAB ZAQ ARAQ RAZAQ

You can do this until you enter a state of deep gnosis. Then the adept to touch both mirrors, creating a magnetic triangle, where the Qliphothic essence of A'rab Zaraq resonates through the black mirror into the ordinary mirror, and also into the adept, acting as a portal to the ingress of such primigenian forces.

The space between both mirrors is the point of nexus, or neither-neither sphere, where the adept can enter into trance and perceive the shadows of A'rab Zaraq with the subconscious mind. It's more than clear that the principal purpose of this ritual is to reflect the shadow from A'rab Zaraq and from the tunnels of the other side, to produce an attractive primigenian gate that can be able to promote the concentration of the adept in a process that aims to transition the adept into a state of high consciousness, through the union and dispersion of the astral realms of A'rab Zaraq.

The Negativity Of Netzach And Darkside Of Venus

Netzach is the seventh sephira, and the first of the third triad. Its nature represents the victory and triumph over the forces of rebellion. Also Netzach represents the instincts and the emotions under its macrocosmic and microcosmic aspects, not forgetting that we are in a sphere of illusion, and that what will be described in terms of form are no more than appearances perceived by the spirit and projected as thought forms in the astral light.

The forces of Netzach are strongly connected with the influence of the planet venus and represents the passions, emotions that the adept must work deeply to not fall into the veils of illusions of emotional shadows that stop the spiritual development.

In Roman mythology Lucifer was the divinity of light and knowledge (in Latin means "bearer of light"), associated with the planet Venus. Its Greek equivalent was Heosphoros or Phosphorus. Venus is the brightest visible star after the sun and moon, and Because its orbit is visible to the east in the last three hours before dawn, Hence the ancients considered that it announced or "carried" the light of the sun. Venus is also visible to the west in the last three hours before nightfall, but the ancient Greeks thought at first that it was another star which they named Hesperus, the Romans called it Vesper and mythologically was Lucifer's brother.

Venus is the planet whose relationship and influence on Earth is the most prominent because according to the occult doctrine, that planet is the firstborn of our Earth, and its spiritual prototype. Every planet has its progenitor star and its sister planet. Hence the Earth is the adopted daughter and younger sister of Venus, but its inhabitants are of its own kind That is that although Venus has a very important occult role in the formation of the Earth, the beings that inhabit the Earth do not come from Venus and have their own evolution. Through this strong connection between adept and venus through the negativity of Netzach and the false victory over instincts of man, the adept is strongly initiated into the mysteries of sacred sexuality and directly associated to the dark side of venus, developing in the subsconsious and transforming the adept in a vessel to gather the black eggs of A´rab Zaraq and through the alchemical process of Nigredo the adept is touched by the turbulents waters of the void and the sacred fire of the ravens of death in a state of developing the depths of the subconscious into the waters of passion of venus, madness of Netzach and death of A'rab Zaraq. In this porcess the adept connects with the Raven of A'arab Zaraq who is stronge associated with death and desintigration, and the hidden path that connects A'rab Zaraq and Thagirion. That path symbolize the transformation and rebirth and is represented by the Atu XIII, the death.

Through the dark side of venus the Adept walks to the gate of astral tunnels of A'arab Zaraq, reflecting its compulsive passion and emotions transforming them in spiritual enlightment. The working of the adept into the negativity of Netzach, prepare him/her to an initiation in the mysteries to devour the astral carrion, symbolizing a form of predatory absorsion of qliphothic powers in this case strongly connected with death and necromancy, due the nature of the qlipha A'rab Zaraq. Through this, the adept solidifies the inner power and transform his/her mind and spirit and flesh in a vessel Which gives the adept the pure essence and the sacred knowledge of the gnosis of death and a certain technique and power to feel the essence of the acausal current. The adept must be careful and not abuse the influences of this qlipha since they have a destructive aspect and he/she should understand that throughout the process he experienced the currents of death flowing through his being.

The Fetish Totem Of A'rab Zaraq (Consecration Rite)

The power of fetish totem of A'rab Zaraq can be activated through sacrifices of blood and the use of tobacco and is magically used for protection, causing harm, increasing wealth or unblock. The Fetish totem must be build with clay, raven or other carrion feathers, and bones. This powerful totem fetish help us within the contact of the adept within the acausal currents of A'rab zaraq and the kingdom of the death. The fetish totem will be done using your creativity, the important here is the focused will through the creation, desire and imagination in order to represent it from elements from your depth consciousness. Is important to know that the fetish must have a small hole on its back in order to include cemetery dust, ashes and everything connected within the death. The baths with rum or any other liquor must be one on saturday after midnight, the same goes for tobacco blowing. Unless you need to do an specific working.

Once the totem fetish is done, put on your altar and let's procceds to have a black candle in front burning properly, representing the black flame balancing you through the kingdom of A'rab Zaraq. Burn some franquisence around the fetish totem in order it absorbs the essence of it. Get a vessel and include on it wine, human or animal bone dust, cemetery soil. Get your dagger and cut your left hand finger and add some drops of blood upon the vessel. Hold the dagger with both hands, touch the fetish totem and cry :

RAB ZAQ ARAQ RAZAQ

RAB ZAQ ARAQ RAZAQ

RAB ZAQ ARAQ RAZAQ

Visualize a strong flux of purple energy from the dagger to the fetish totem and proclaims :

By the mystery of Veiled Mask of A'rab Zaraq

The Gates of the void, and the Dark Threshold

I Place the Sacramental Fire Upon the Sacred Arte

Into the Hidden Sanctuary of Necrosophic gnosis

May all the Powers of Raven's Venomous Seal

Absorbed by the Secret Tongue of Qayin

Under the 13th palace of Baa'l I Zaraq

Awakening the Powers of the Hidden Tunnel of Niantiel

The Adept got the tobacco and blow 13 times upon the fetish while visualizing a black flux of energy emerging from the smocke of the tobacco to the fetish totem and cry :

RAB ZAQ ARAQ RAZAQ

RAB ZAQ ARAQ RAZAQ

RAB ZAQ ARAQ RAZAQ

Start to masturbate him / herself slowly and proclaims:

Within the Blessings of the Immortal fire

God of the Void, Death and Carrion

Raven of Dispersion, Destroyer of Worlds

Invisible Claw of the Hidden Tunnel

Primal Ravenous God

I Call forth the Vaccum of Blackned Light

The Raven of the Death, The Raven of the Carrion

Give Me the Strenght and Power to Consecrate This

Fetish Totem In Its Name

A'rab Zaraq, My libations are for you

A'rab Zaraq, My flesh to you

A'rab Zaraq, Be the Primal Force of the Void

A'rab Zaraq, Be thy Blood In My Veins

At the point of orgasm cry :

RAB ZAQ ARAQ RAZAQ

RAB ZAQ ARAQ RAZAQ

RAB ZAQ ARAQ RAZAQ

Put the sexual fluids on the vessel and mix it properly, and procceds to bath the fetish with its contens and proclaims :

> By the Turbulent waters of the chaos
>
> Whose Primal source is the Essence of Death
>
> I invoke the Powers of Transformation
>
> I invoke the Powers of Transmigration
>
> I invoke the Powers of The Raven of Dispersion
>
> To give power to this Totem fetish
>
> To be a Nexion Between the Adept and
>
> The Kingdom of Death & Carrion
>
> Open a Sinister Path of Wisdom and Power

Meditate for some minutes and visualize, a purple light ascending from your lower chakra to the Ajna one. Cover the fetish totem in a black clothe and close the ritual. Let the black candle burning until its estinguish.

The Obsidian Gate And The Nigredo Phase

The Obsidian gate is the entrance to the connection within the current of A'rab Zaraq through the process of Nigredo, that leads the adept into the descomposition and spiritual death, to reborn and complete the backward path to connect with this qlipha. The transformation through inner fire of Nigredo reduced the body and soul of the adept to its primal state from which it originally arose when started the voyage inside the tunnels of the qlipha A'rab Zaraq. The Obsidian gate vitalizes the purpose of the soul, eliminates blockages when the adept is trascending the passing through the qlipha A'rab Zaraq and open deep channels of perception, integrating the psychological shadow with the whole to produce spiritual integrity. Connects through a strong way, the spirit in the body when the adept is moving to astral temples of the raven of dispersion. This gate stimulates growth at all levels, encourages to explore the unknown paths of the qlipha opening new astral temples for future explorations.

In qliphotic alchemy, the black flame through the disintegration and spiritual death that goes and surround the image of the head of the raven representing A'arab zaraq, receive the name of nigredo. This stage of sinister alchemical process reflects the disintegration of the soul of the adept moving into astral projections, and guide us to learn how to understand its essential components, which can only be achieved by the process of putrefaction. Nigredo simply means blackening. Without Nigredo there is no possibility that the adept can be transformed, since it must first be stripped, purified and reduced to its magickal essence, something that can not be achieved without putrefaction and death. Without nigredo there is no possibility of anything new. When the adept is stripped of the mask, what remains is the skull, of A'rab Zaraq the caput mortuum.

When applying the concept of Nigredo into the works within A'rab Zaraq, we sail in an ocean of evolution and primal transformation of consciousness. The nigredo is necessary, and must precceds the more advanced stages of the process. It reflects the problem of being immersed in the experience of mortality and the dark world of shadow that now represents our own mastery of diverse emotions through a deep confrontation and the dispersion of our own being. Often, when the adept walk the path of the raven of dispersion the adept awkens an inner balance and power to conquer the diverse elements reached through the Nigredo phase.

Speaking in a symbolic language Nigredo reflects in its psychological key the internal struggles of the human soul, we see it through the tasks and trials of the adept have to trascends. He /she is the one who has enough courage to face himself, to see his monsters, his fears, without projecting them on others in an attitude to run away from the truth that he can not recognize. The adept is precisely because he sees himself as he is, without veils, masks or disguises, and his capacity for struggle represents his / her inner strength applied in the process of transformation of his /her personality.

The victory achieved will be the result of this process of internal struggle and transmutation of defects with which we depart, by virtues conquered on the basis of effort, perseverance and self-confidence, as well as value applied daily to daily walking into the obsidian gates opening to see face to face A'rab zaraq and to die and reborn from the ashes, now trasnformed into a primal vessel incubating and generating all the power connected within this qlipha, through self mastery, dedication and self experience. There is always empowering beyond the darkness that envelops us at any given moment, but we must advance with courage and determination, with strong will focused through the black flame that we reach beyond the primal path of A'rab Zaraq.

The Sanctuary Of The Raven's Flesh (Invocation)

The follow invocation is a depth calling of the shadow realsm of the ravens of dispersion, in the flesh of the adept having as principal point, the focus of the essence of the qlipha to assist the adept to unblock the energies that stop the ascending through the tree of death and developing the depths of the subconscious creating a perfect nexion between the adept and the qlipha A'rab Zaraq.

In front of your altar, burn frankisence incense and burn a black candle and put on the sigil of the qlipha in front of the Fetish totem. Visualize deeply the sigil while chanting the mantra

RAB ZAQ ARAQ RAZAQ

RAB ZAQ ARAQ RAZAQ

RAB ZAQ ARAQ RAZAQ

After some minutes follow the invocation:

Baal I Zaraq, I Invoke the powers of War and Death

To Walk the Therionic Paths of the shadows and Flesh

A'rab Zaraq, Thou Who Transform My Flesh In Carrion

Who Drinks the nectars of my poisonus Soul, In the Vessel of the Void

RAB ZAQ ARAQ RAZAQ

RAB ZAQ ARAQ RAZAQ

RAB ZAQ ARAQ RAZAQ

Hail thou!! Oh, God With blackned Wings and Empty Eyes

Carry Me to the Labyrinths of Your Secret Temples

And Teach Me, the Sacred Gnosis Now forgotten

Tear My Soul With Your Poisonous claws

RAB ZAQ ARAQ RAZAQ

RAB ZAQ ARAQ RAZAQ

RAB ZAQ ARAQ RAZAQ

Devour My Soul With your Tongue of Fire

Makes Me One With Your Primal Essence

Oh, Baa'l I Zaraq Oh, A'rab Zaraq

Whose Throne is Made of Black Obsidian Stone

And The Crown Full of Bones and Ashes

RAB ZAQ ARAQ RAZAQ

RAB ZAQ ARAQ RAZAQ

RAB ZAQ ARAQ RAZAQ

Oh, My winged God, Delight at Invisible Gardens

Devours my Soul, In The Sanctuary of Flesh

Keys to Infinite Madness

Nightsidepaths, Quintessence of Flesh

Sanctuary of the Void, Essence of the Death

Illuminator and Poison Spirit

Prince of Death and War

Open to Me the Path and Flesh

To your Hidden Sanctuary of the Void

RAB ZAQ ARAQ RAZAQ

RAB ZAQ ARAQ RAZAQ

RAB ZAQ ARAQ RAZAQ

Let's procceds to meditate for some minutes and feel how the essence of the Qlipha is slowly penetrating your flesh, body and soul and focus all energy to awaken the power of the Qlipha within yourself. And close he ritual chamber

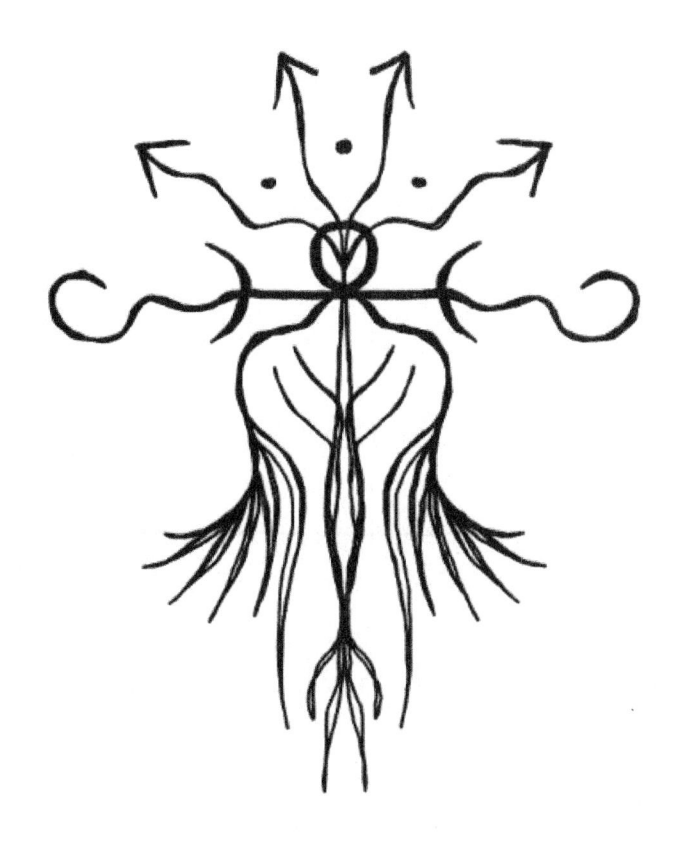

Sigil Of A'rab Zaraq

Theriomorphic Shadow Of Baal I Zaraq

Baal means prince and the name of that Canaanite divinity with powers of augur was Baal Zebul, venerated in Ecron, one of the five great philistine cities. That old and respected god fell into disgrace, made him devil, and came to dwell in the most sinister abyss of sheol. His name was transcribed into Hebrew as Baal-zebub, meaning lord of the flies, probably for raising the contemptuous tinge of pagan divinity and relating it, as to these insects, to putrefaction and death. Baal is strongly connected with wars and inner battles of the adept to destroy the elements who limits its evolution.

Baal is the guide who lead us to the hidden rites of necromancy in this qlipha, and when due its strongly connected with A'rab Zaraq, emerges a strong theriomorphic current of self liberation through spiritual death that the adept must explore to trascends death itself in order to ascend from ashes in a magickal rebirth. This unión gives the adept the knowledge to work in diverse rituals focusing the necrosophic gnosis and is here where you can find Baa'l I Zaraq as a guardian guide, liberating the soul of the adept through the spiritual death and be crowned by the black light of the ravens of dispersión.

Through all this process of descomposition in the shadows of Baa'l I Zaraq, the adept enter through its own shadow as a warrior fighting the elements he needs in order to trascends, to transform his/ her soul through violence, courage and balance, to keep on moving into the qlipha with the necessary power and undestanding to trascends the limits of madness and death due the nature of the qlipha.

Each exploration will give to the adept a determinate technic power to feel the force of the acausal current of the qlipha. The adept must be carefully when exploring the diverse methods, he / she will experience the destructive and hateful shadows of Baa'l I Zaraq, the knowledge gotten through the explorations offer the adept, a sigil that condenses his / her energy in the psysical, astral, spiritual, and mental fields. The sigil can be used as a powerful vessel of connection within the qlipha that helps to understand the mysteries of necromantic explorations handled through Theriomorphic shadow of Baa'l I Zaraq. The introspection and proper understanding of the essence of Baa'l I Zaraq reveals the adept the gnosis of nigredo as a powerful path full of thorns and bones into the 11 gates of amenti.

Explorations Of Tunnels Of Niantiel & Kurgasiax

Niantel is the guardian of 24th tunnel and is the master of death, the trickster, warrior, and the personal messenger of the destiny of the adept when exploring the path of A'rab Zaraq. He has the power to remove the obstacles and he provides opportunities to the adpet when focusing deeply into the tunnel itself. All ceremonies developed though this tunnel need of the invocation of Niantiel. This is the guardian that makes us transcend the limits of the tunnel, unifying with the forces of Kurgasiax creating a link between the physical plane and the reality beyond the tunnels itself. But at the same time, it is a primordial and acausal force, hence in many rituals, the visions are confusing for many adepts who explore the death cults due the convergences of dark plutonian energies of transformation and regeneration that the adept must explore in order to absorb the energy of the tunnel and can visualize the path when moving through the webs of A'rab Zaraq.

Niantiel occupies an important point when exploring the qlipha A'rab Zaraq and is invoked for very practical purposes, since it has to do with the seas of death and the natural cycles of change and trasnformation, it is a guardian of the tunnel but it is also who governs the emotions, the intuition and the astral plane connected with the qlipha. Something very interesting that I see in this is the conjoining of both tunnels Niantiel and Kurgasiax, that is to say on the one hand, we have the acausal visions of a raven that comes from the abyssal waters of death, and on the other hand, we have a much more elemental invocation of its energy applied towards a much more practical end such as getting direction of the emotions while exploring the tunnel. I think this tunnel has to do with disbalance, with death of the adept in the claws of the qlipha and through an alchemical process of putrefaction, to came life in the womb of the void itself absorbing its energy and seek its guidance to produce a change in our reality through the focused will.

Through Kurgasiax the adept reborn as a new individual awakening diverse elements who help him / her to the transit into other paths and tunnels. Kurgasiax represents controlled raw strength and power, the Adept who explore this tunnel must have a desired goal to achieve, thus the ends to materialize it. Through a proper exploration Kurgasiax as the primal guardian of the tunnel, also represents literal warfare and violence, is the blade which cuts without mercy the negative elements of the adept and his/ her limitations in a ways as the adept can reflect him/ herself in the turbulent waters of death in order to reflect his/ her own will and to focus in the exploration of the tunnel itself.

Final Word: The Sphere Of Unstoppable Intention

Working in the current of the Qliphoth is intense. The forces and energies that reside there are so incredibly strong and demand much of the black magician. The realm of the Sitra Ahra is not for one weak of mind or spirit, the intelligences there temper the black magician, fine tune them to achieve greater success within their Personal Reality Grid. The Qliphoth truly purify, remove unneeded doubt and fear, and refine their focus. Passing through each of the Qliphothic spheres on the Tree of Death is a personal pathworking I think each black magician should work through at least once in their life, as a sort of rite of passage.

The Qlipha A'arab-Zaraq is one of the most powerful shells on the Tree of Death. It is for those who need results and change immediately, with no regard of consequences to others. These beings fight amongst themselves as piranha feasting. Nothing matters but self and obtaining the end result, whatever that may be. This energy burns bright and fast, as a star explodes in the night sky, quickly and intensely. Working with this sphere wears on the black magician over a short period of time. The work done with this sphere must have focus and Intent.

I wish the black magician who decides to wield this grimoire safe passage. May the forces spoken of herein not ravage their life, and tear them asunder…

~ S. Ben Qayin

~ S. Ben Qayin ~

I have researched and practiced various forms of magic throughout my lengthy course of esoteric study, working in many areas of Ceremonial Magic. However, I discovered early on that magic was a thread that was woven through all things, and so was drawn to more personalized Chaos Magic from a young age. I hold the belief that magic is not 'magical', that it does not 'just happen', nor is it 'miraculous', I see it as a scientific system based on a process that we have yet to fully understand scientifically. This is based on my concept that humans do not fully realize the base structure of their reality in which they are currently residing, and that they have yet to understand all the rules of the 'Consensual Reality Matrix', and therefore do not entirely understand or utilize their personal energy and influence within it. I view magic as the manipulation of personal energy to restructure or influence the 'Consensual Reality Matrix' to conform to the Intent of the magician. As with all energy, I believe magic can be harnessed and directed, spirits and entities can be contacted, and change can be made manifest within 'The Personal Reality Grid' of the magician. I can assist you to unlock this hidden potential.

As the previous Head of the Inner Order of the Voltec, I have had years of training in shifting my perception of reality, and thus am able to successfully manipulate the 'Structure'. The Order of the Voltec were an offshoot from

The Temple of Set, which of course is an offshoot from LaVey's Church of Satan.

Chaos magic or 'Fringe Magic' as I refer to it, is not new. It is simply a category or term created to encompass scientific magic or magic that deals with dimensions, non-human intelligences and work that questions the basis of reality, and how to manipulate it. This can be classified as experimental magic, teetering on the edge of the abyss of creation. Of course, Fringe Magic does encompass such literary works from authors and magicians who have ventured forth into the empty spaces, such as H.P. Lovecraft, Carlos Castaneda, Pete Carroll, Frank G. Ripel, Michael Bertiaux, Kenneth Grant and others who have been to the edge of creation and reality, and returned to write of it. They have masterfully transformed into words, experiences and concepts that are seemingly indescribable to those who have not walked the 'Spaces In-Between' themselves, who have not known the 'Twilight of Being and Reality'.

I Have Written:

"Volubilis Ex Chaosium"

"The Book Of Smokeless Fire"

"Harab Serapel; The Ravens Of The Burning God"

"The Black Book Of Azathoth"

"Thaumiel; The Dark Divided Ones"

"The Book Of Smokeless Fire II; Into The Crucible"

"S. Ben Qayin; The Collected Writings"

Contact Me Here:

Website: www.SBenQayin.com

Email: S.BenQayin@ymail.com

FaceBook: S Ben Qayin